Tricia Guild in town

Contemporary design for urban living

Photography - Gilles de Chabaneix

Text - Elspeth Thompson

Quadrille

For S.J. and S.J.

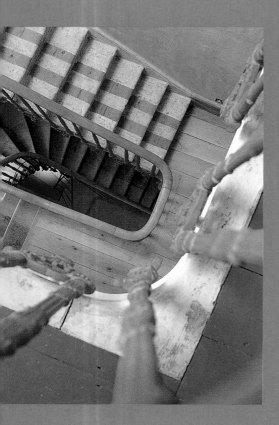

Publishing Director Anne Furniss
Design Meryl Lloyd
Tricia Guild's Creative Assistant Jo Willer
Production Vincent Smith

First published in 1996 by
Quadrille Publishing Limited
9 Irving Street, London WC2H 7AT

British Library Cataloguing in Publication Data
A catalogue record for this book is available from
the British Library
ISBN 1 899988 16 5

Typesetting & Artwork by R&B Creative Services

Printed and bound by Mohndruck Graphische
Betriebe GmbH, Germany

Special thanks to those who have generously allowed us to photograph their homes – Richard Polo for our house – Simon and Alison Jeffreys for their colourful town house – Lisa Guild for her serene apartment – Maureen Missner and John Venema for their artistic brownstone – Jo Willer for her charming cottage – Mark Homewood for his dynamic apartment and loft – June and Jon Summerill for their precious studio in Paris.

I would also like to thank – Gilles de Chabaneix for his glorious photography and Richard Boutin who assists – Elspeth Thompson for capturing the spirit with her elegant writing – Meryl Lloyd for her constant support and superb design – Anne Furniss and Alison Cathie at Quadrille – Alfred Munkenbeck and his assistant Juan Dols for minimalism – The Designers Guild team before, during and after this book was produced – Jo Willer who assists me brilliantly with my work.

Contents

Foreword

The creation of a home, a private special world in which to live, in my view can be like searching for a more vivid existence, whether it be brilliant minimalist architecture, a period town house, loft or studio. Embracing the dynamic tensions of the city is both fascinating and daunting, full of promise and potential. It is the idealist who takes on the challenge.

Changing the interior of our house from its original role as a traditional town house to that of a contemporary living environment, combined with our wish to live in a space that is both minimal and simultaneously inspiring, generous and full of vitality, presented us with just such a challenge: all encompassing, yet ultimately immensely satisfying. It has been said that one's domestic environment is a reflection of one's character. Initially, one searches for the concept, formulates the vision, then tackles the vital practical issues. The process of confronting and solving problems, meeting deadlines, taking courageous decisions can be soul searching, painful, but fulfilling. That same process is echoed when working with like-minded people, helping to stimulate their dream-making potential.

I hope that these pages capture the vision. They attempt to reflect the valuable, emotionally satisfying process of making individual spaces that are not finished, static objects but which continue to move and grow with our lives.

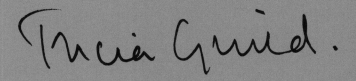

'Men came together in cities in
order to live. They remain together
in order to enjoy the good life.'
Aristotle, *Politics*, 4th century BC

Rejoice in

Say the word 'city' and what do you see? A bustling street market, the air thick with traders' cries and

neighbourly gossip? The hub of the financial quarter, bristling with tall glass towers and men in dark suits? Or

a sunny Sunday in the park, the city's inhabitants slumped in rows of striped deckchairs, while streams of

children and dogs weave a procession in between?

Perhaps you see a city from history: Rome under the Emperors, the St Petersburg of the Tsars, or the

pinnacles of some timeless, nameless city of the East, arising from the desert like a mirage. Or maybe you see

it through the eyes of a writer or a painter: Dickens's London, Baudelaire's or Manet's Paris, the luminous

anonymity of Hopper's late-night bars, the wit and angst of Woody Allen's New York. Generations of artists

have found in the city a potent metaphor for the human condition: for its splendour and its squalor, for our

sociability as well as our fundamental loneliness, for fortunes to be made, dreams fulfilled and forgotten.

the city

Cities have always been exciting places to live, full of contrasts and extremes. Ever since the first cities were raised from the Middle-eastern mud, they have acted as magnets for the agents of change and renewal; marketplaces for the exchange of new ideas as well as a trade in goods and services. Cradles of our civilization, they have been seedbeds of revolution in everything from politics and philosophy to art and architecture, fashion and entertainment.

Modernity and change are woven into the fabric of city life. The way most cities grow is organic – sprawling and contracting, different neighbourhoods rising and falling – continually adapting themselves to the demands of their inhabitants. Old buildings may be pulled down and new ones put up, but the past is never erased; it is there to be traced in the name of a street, the carving above a doorway, an old pub sign. Ancient and modern coexist – as do beautiful and ugly, rich and poor, sociability and alienation – often within the space of a single street.

Common criticisms of the city are that it is noisy, polluted and dangerous, and there is no doubt that this century's emphasis on economic expansion, and in particular the rise of the motor car, have done nothing to enhance its allure. All too often, urban living is regarded as a compromise – convenience and accessibility constantly weighed against the disadvantages of congestion, uniformity, chaos and grime. Town and country can become polarised in our imaginations until the countryside has a monopoly on space, on solace, on soul. But it doesn't have to be that way.

Problems there may be, but there has seldom been a more exciting time to live in the city. Recent years have seen something of an urban renaissance take root throughout much of the western world, from splendid public art and architecture projects in Paris, Stuttgart and Seattle to the redomestication of parts of the financial districts of London and New York. Contemporary parks and river walkways are opening up brave new urban vistas everywhere from Barcelona to Newcastle. Measures are being considered to fight pollution, and some cities are already leading the way in curbing car use and creating energy-efficient new transport systems. The architect Richard Rogers is one among many who are striving to realise a new vision of city living – sustainable in economic, cultural and psychological terms – that can take us into the next century and beyond.

The time has come to celebrate the city and to find new ways of living in it. The key to urban living is to rejoice in urban virtues. Let go of the rural idyll: the need for friends and flexibility, for constant change and challenge, that the city fulfils can be as crucial to wellbeing as acres of unadulterated green. From elegant town houses and cosy mews cottages, to docklands warehouses and rooftop eyries with chimneyscape views, the city offers an exciting variety of living spaces. More recently, former industrial buildings are being converted into stylish new loft apartments, providing exciting expanses of space at affordable prices, right in the centre of town. All of these can easily be adapted to fit a modern way of life.

The city home is an ideal place to develop a new definition of modernity. No retro nostalgia here, no rural hankerings in the form of dried flowers in your kitchen and wall-to-wall chintz. You don't need a modern

'The city does not tell its past, but contains it like the lines of a hand, written in the corners of the streets, the gratings of the windows, the bannisters of the steps, the antennae of the lightning rods, the poles of the flags ...'
Italo Calvino, *Invisible Cities,* 1972

'Cities have changed so much that it is hard to remember they exist first and foremost for people ... We should be reinvesting in the idea of a dense and socially diverse city ... focusing communities around lively neighbourhoods.'
Richard Rogers, *The Reith Lectures,* 1995

house to have a modern home; all you need is a modern attitude. When decorating, don't deny the city; rather, distil the best of its essence and bring it inside. Think of the way a city grows: of the organic mixture of old and new, of the exciting melting pot of cultures – and reflect this in the arrangement of space, the choice of materials, the incorporation of contemporary arts and crafts. Let your home resound to the rhythms of the city. While a country house is about long, lazy weekends, home life in town is knitted into the fabric of the city and shares its constant comings and goings. It needs to be accessible and adaptable, able to open up for an impromptu summer lunch party, but also to provide a peaceful haven from the pace and pressures of the world outside.

This new vision of urban living is about much more than mere decorating – it is part of the general shift in attitudes that is affecting us all as we edge towards the end of the century. Just as in fashion, where padded shoulders and power dressing are now a thing of the past, the mood in interior design is also moving towards something softer, more soulful, and much more individual. Making a home is not a matter of what you put on your walls or how you hang your curtains. It is an emotional response to your surroundings and the way you want to live. For Tricia Guild, it is also where she experiments with the colours and textures, forms and ideas that will inspire her next collection of fabrics and furniture.

For twenty-five years, as the founding director and creative force behind Designers Guild, Tricia Guild has been at the cutting edge of contemporary interior design. Her innate ability to mix vibrant colour and pattern and her imaginative use of modern arts and crafts translate particularly well to the challenges of urban living. A passionate urbanite, who flies frequently between the world's capitals, she rejoices in the rich visual stimulation and dynamic energy of the city. Her country house in the hills of Tuscany is a beautiful refuge for relaxing with her family, but London is her longterm home. It is also the international base for Designers Guild, from the bright and busy shops in the heart of the King's Road, Chelsea, to the converted Victorian printworks north of Holland Park that houses the creative team, sales, finance and production staff. Tricia Guild's new London house, a short walk from the office and within easy reach of the lively antique

markets, museums and galleries, smart restaurants and street theatre that animate the city, is the perfect illustration of her vision of urban living.

On the following pages, a tour of Tricia Guild's house shows how using the inspiration of the city can create the ultimate urban home. Visits to a variety of other city homes she has decorated or helped to inspire – all owned by like-minded people who share her vision of city life – demonstrate that the ideas can be adapted to very different spaces, from a family town house to a tiny artisan's cottage, a New York apartment block to a Parisian pied-à-terre, the perfect one-person hideaway to the skyline sanctuary of a brand-new London loft.

'It's all about old meeting new.
Very few people build a new
house in the city – one chooses a
certain space with a certain
character and the challenge is to
dance off that character, adding
individuality in the process.'
Tricia Guild

A space in the city
Tricia Guild's London home

Tricia Guild's London house is the ultimate illustration of her new definition of modernity. It is also perfect proof that you don't need a brand-new building in order to create a totally modern living space. Just as in the ever-changing modern city, old and new coexist in a series of exciting contrasts – the spire of a medieval church reflected in a skyscraper's sheet-glass windows, a piece of modern sculpture animating an old cobbled street – Tricia Guild has taken this strong urban mixture and made it part of the very fabric of her home. Her radical transformation of a large Victorian family house did not begin with a ruthless ripping out of its traditional features; nor, of course, has it involved a thoughtless veneration of the past. Instead, an exciting tension between old and new runs through the house like an electric current.

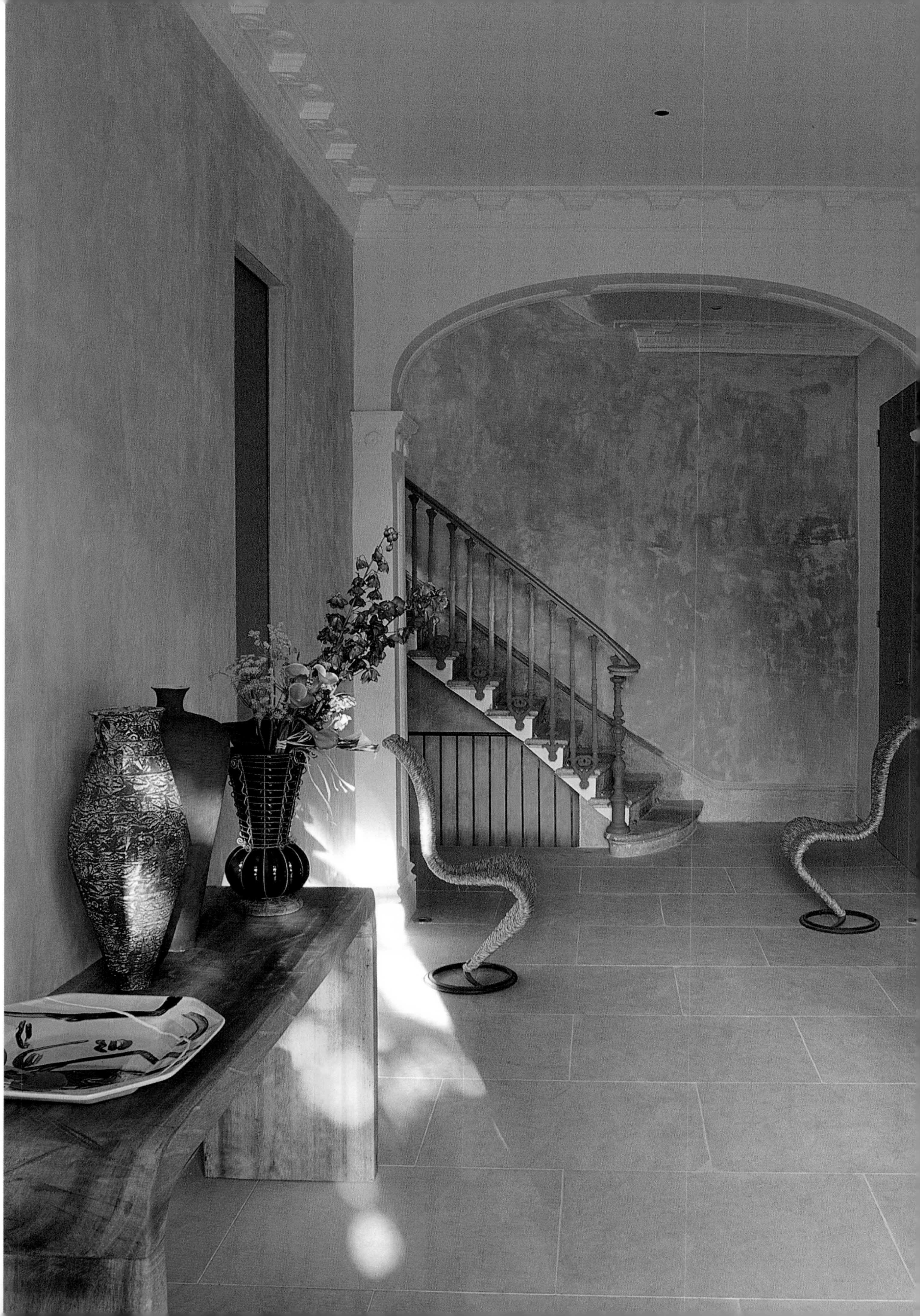

The bright, airy entrance hall sets the scene with its exciting combination of old-meets-new. Walls the swirling colour and texture of a contemporary abstract painting butt up against original cornices, their convoluted mouldings painted crisp white, like the icing on a wedding cake. Traditional arched windows are left bare, their plaster surrounds suffused with zingy lime green, to make sunny niches for contemporary arts and crafts; modern ceramics and sculptural flowers create a warm but unusual welcome.

At the very heart of the house, the original freestanding staircase, its ornate iron balusters painted a flaming orange, provides the strongest visual metaphor for the fantastic fusion of old and new that runs throughout the house. At the top, a plain round glass skylight throws ellipses of light around the stairwell, marking the passage of time like an interior sundial.

light

colour

texture

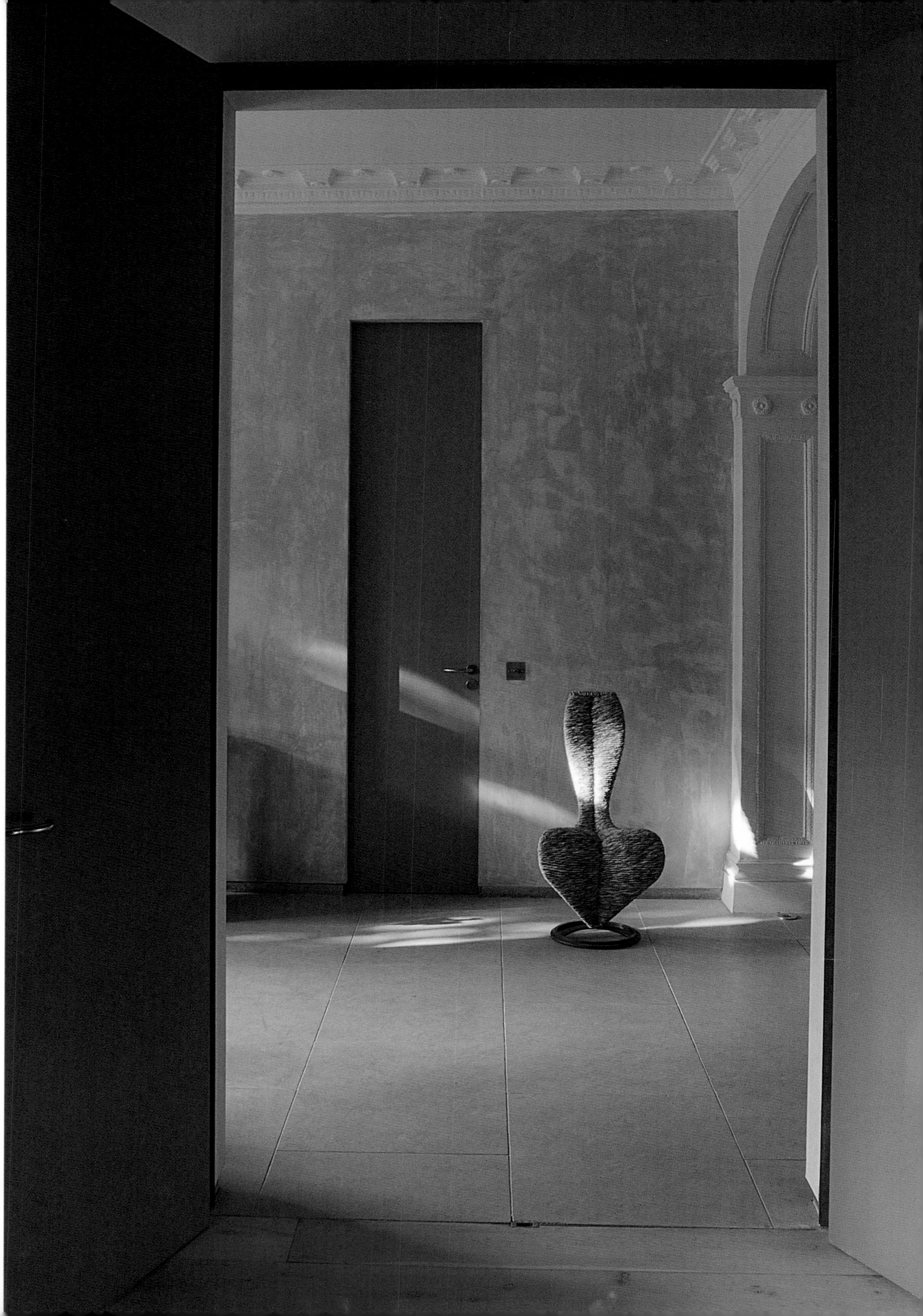

Still in the entrance hall, tall, narrow
doorways accentuate the natural elegance
of the house's proportions. A raffia chair
by Tom Dixon stands sentinel at the entrance
to the downstairs lavatory – a tiny space
brought alive by cobalt-blue mosaic tiles,
contemporary arts and crafts and a single,
sloping sheet of glass that makes an
intriguing wash-basin.

tall doorways, open space

Off the hallway, the airy, glass-roofed studio/conservatory is where Tricia Guild comes to work and think as the ever-changing light throws patterns around the bright blue walls. Neither indoors nor out, the room opens onto small terraces at both the front and the back of the house, and can be looked down on from the arched stairwell window.

Like many others in the house, the studio walls are suffused with swirling colour, applied to the raw plaster while it was still wet. They make a dynamic backdrop for favourite books and treasures, such as ceramics, embroidered textiles, plants and flowers collected for inspiration. In summer, an armchair and table can be taken outside for a view over the garden.

sunlight through glass

organic

patina

ceramic

crafted

handsewn

indigo

orange

The studio/conservatory is an example of how one can create new and exciting spaces while still remaining sensitive to a building's original architecture. From the front of the house, there are few signs that such a thoroughly modern room exists behind the sunny roof terrace. Slanting slashes of glass in the roof make for maximum light all year round, while preserving the privacy that is so vital to life in the city. Here, one of the glass panels butts up against the arched window in the stairwell, framing a view down onto Tricia Guild's private world.

Space to live in

Old houses were built for a very different way of life. Until recently, large houses, both rural and urban, tended to have different rooms for specific purposes: drawing rooms and dining rooms, parlours and pantries – not to mention nurseries, sculleries and servants' quarters. For most of us, life in the modern age is much less structured, and some degree of adaptation is usually necessary to make a successful contemporary home. Some of the latest urban architectural developments – from the conversion of an old Parisian train station into the Musée d'Orsay to the transformation of former riverside warehouses into flats and restaurants along London's Butlers' Wharf – suggest how sensitivity to the past can go hand in hand with stunning modernity. In Tricia Guild's house, respect for the generous solidity of the mid-Victorian architecture has not prevented the opening up of the interior almost to the limits of structural feasibility, while new spaces, such as a book-lined study and the studio/conservatory, have also been created.

When Tricia Guild and her husband came across this house, like so many larger town houses it had been converted into flats, its graceful proportions clumsily carved up into small compartments. Despite this, she could see the potential to open up the original larger space and create an almost minimalist canvas which she could then colour in and bring to life. The result is a stimulating environment that is at once of the city, reflecting its exciting cultural rhythms, but also apart from it; a place that can accommodate large-scale entertaining as well as informal family life; a dynamic backdrop for contemporary arts and crafts and, in the new studio/conservatory she has created, a reflective space in which she could explore the rich sensuality of her thoughts about colour and texture, recharge her creative batteries and make room for new ideas to surface and distil into form.

Consulting and working with Alfred Munkenbeck, an architect whose views on the simplicity of space and minimalist detailing she shares, the house's interior has now been re-established as four principal living spaces which are much looser in nature than the original occupants would have been used to; an open-plan kitchen-dining room and seating area on the garden floor; an elegant double sitting room, study and conservatory off the hallway on the raised ground floor; the master bedroom, bathroom and dressing rooms occupying the whole of the first floor, and guest bedrooms and bathrooms in the former staff bedrooms up at the top. Changing the position of some of the doorways means the flow of movement now suits a more contemporary way of life. Tall, narrow double doors accentuate the main rooms' dramatic high ceilings; in the bedroom where no elaborate original cornicing remains, these stretch right up to ceiling height. The upper floor bedrooms retain their original atticky charm.

'The house has a strong, organic blend of neutral textures and materials with exciting colour – the two are interfused so that rather than being a distraction, or an end in itself, colour forms part of the texture and pattern and emotion of the space.'
Tricia Guild

Light

On the lower floors of the house, the aim has been not only to open up the interior space itself, but to extend it, both psychologically and visually, out into the gardens at front and back. In earlier times, for safety, comfort and security, houses were designed to shut the door on nature and the elements; these days, particularly in the city, if you are lucky enough to have a green view, it makes sense to bring it indoors. In the kitchen, the coved brick ceilings of what was originally the cellar, held up by the slenderest of steel verticals, stretch all the way from the front wall to the back, which has been replaced by a bank of six galvanized metal and glass doors. Sun streams down through six skylights, throwing lozenges of light onto the pale stone floor; this same surface is continued out into the terraced garden – another device that extends the room beyond its physical dimensions. With steps up and away from the house, bordered with pots spilling over with flowers, the garden provides its own organic screen from neighbours and passers by. In the sitting room upstairs, elegant French windows can be thrown open onto a metalwork balcony overlooking the public gardens beyond, while slashes of glass in the roof of the conservatory/studio open it up to the changing sky. And at the very top of the house, the introduction of a plain round skylight throws welcome shafts of light into the stairwell.

Colour an

Cities are often perceived as grey and soulless, but where there is colour, it sings out all the more against a neutral backdrop. Think of rows of bright vegetables on stalls in a city square, the flashing of neon against a night sky, the peeling layers of film and theatre bills on an old brick wall. The streets are full of inspiration for using colour in the urban home.

Tricia Guild has brought alive the cool, open, almost minimalist framework of her new house with an exciting new fusion of colour and texture – rich and organic but completely contemporary. Seldom is colour seen as a flat, inanimate surface. The walls vibrate with flat swirls of pure pigment sunk into the raw plaster as it dried, or flash with the glint of thousands of tiny mosaic tiles in cobalt blue, lime or orange. On the wooden stairs and top landing, the stripping back of layers of paint suggested an abstract, striped finish – at once strikingly modern and totally in keeping with the original atticky style. In the top bedrooms, asymmetrical plains and stripes blur into one another with all the quiet beauty of a Rothko canvas.

Certain colours recur like themes in a musical score: the lime green of the hall reappears on the far wall

d texture

of the sitting room and again downstairs in the kitchen; warm blues were chosen for the master bedroom and the conservatory; accents of orange run from the kitchen up to the topmost bedroom, their progress followed by the orange staircase itself. There are striking contrasts as coloured walls meet at corners, as a pink room is glimpsed through a lime doorway; as the curlicue arm of a blue chair sings out against a warm pink backdrop. The vibrant mix of colour might seem overpowering were it not for the vital part played by the countering neutrals and naturals.

Tricia Guild's use of bright colour works because it is balanced. The sitting room in this house may be turquoise, but not all the walls have been coloured. There are planes of white plaster which allow the colours to breathe and, paradoxically, increase their impact. The floors are pale stone or bleached wood and the paintwork is either white or a soft blue-grey, creating space and light around windows and doors and making a neutral buffer between rooms and the spaces beyond. Other neutral textures incorporate something of the urban aesthetic: acid-treated zinc in the kitchen fittings and etched glass and brushed chrome in the bathroom have a semi-industrial feel that contrasts well with the painterly use of colour.

cobalt vermilion indigo magenta orange mandarin

'Most people have a strong
personal feeling for colour.
It's important to trust and be
sensitive to one's own
intuitive colour sense –
discovering it is challenging,
stimulating and creates
dynamic and positive energy.'
Tricia Guild

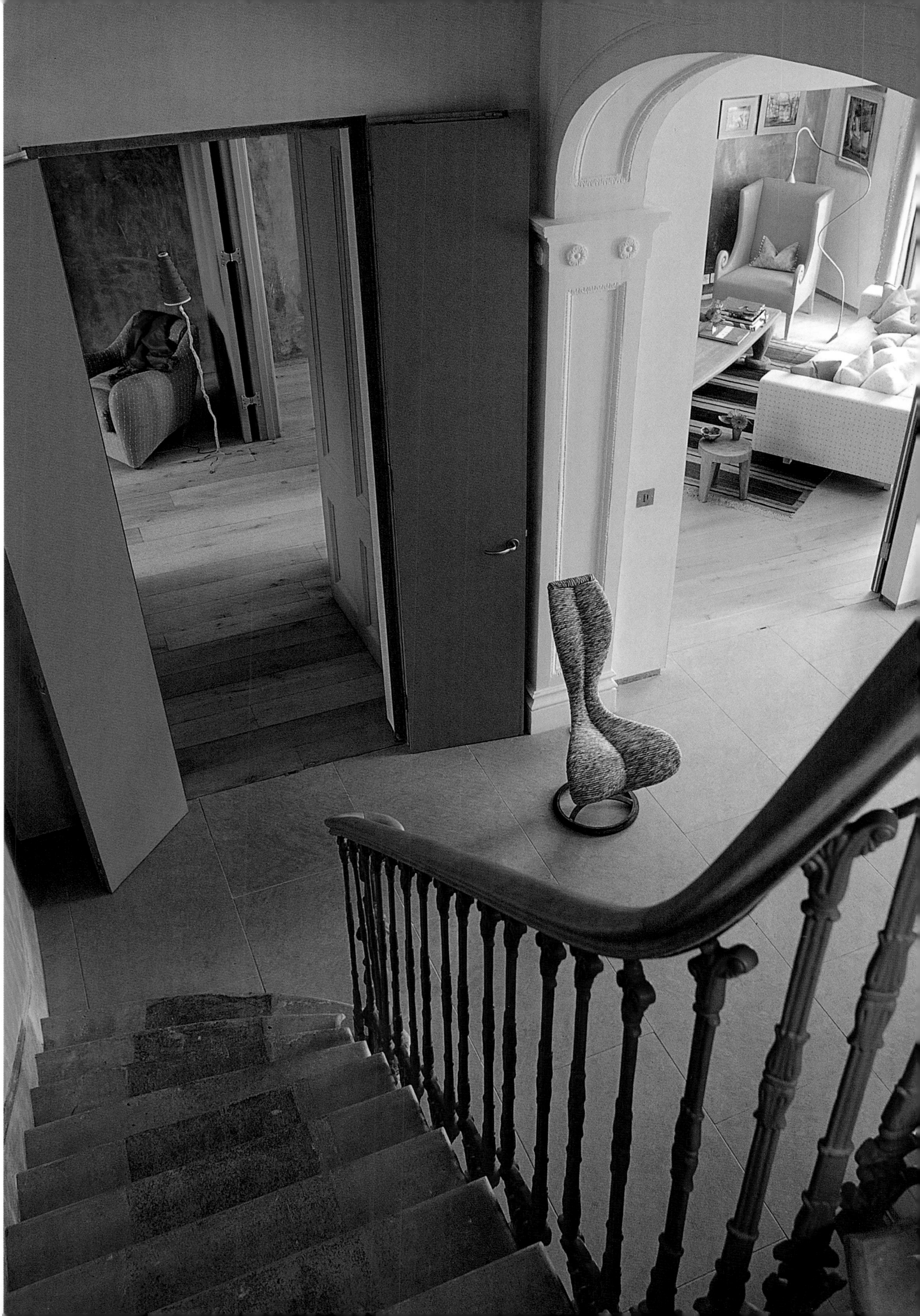

Looking from the hall to the sitting room: a modern mix of colour and texture brings striking individuality to the large double room, while the original crisp cornices and subtle, sculptural pieces of furniture emphasise its elegant proportions. Tricia Guild's use of bright, vibrant colour is balanced by the use of white and neutrals. In the spirit of the Mexican architect Luis Barragan, not all the walls are painted turquoise, and plenty of white around the windows increases the feeling of light. The clean, modern framework has been coloured in with contemporary furniture, arts and crafts. Modern ceramics echo the rich, rubbed-down textures of the stairs and walls, and textiles vary from gold-printed crushed linen to pale natural sackcloth embroidered with string. This is the most formal space in the house, but the unexpected juxtapositions of colours, styles and materials prevent it from becoming remotely stuffy. The urban sitting room is often required to adapt to different situations; Tricia Guild's is equally suited to a large drinks party or a quiet afternoon reading in the calm, diffused light by the window.

relaxed elegance

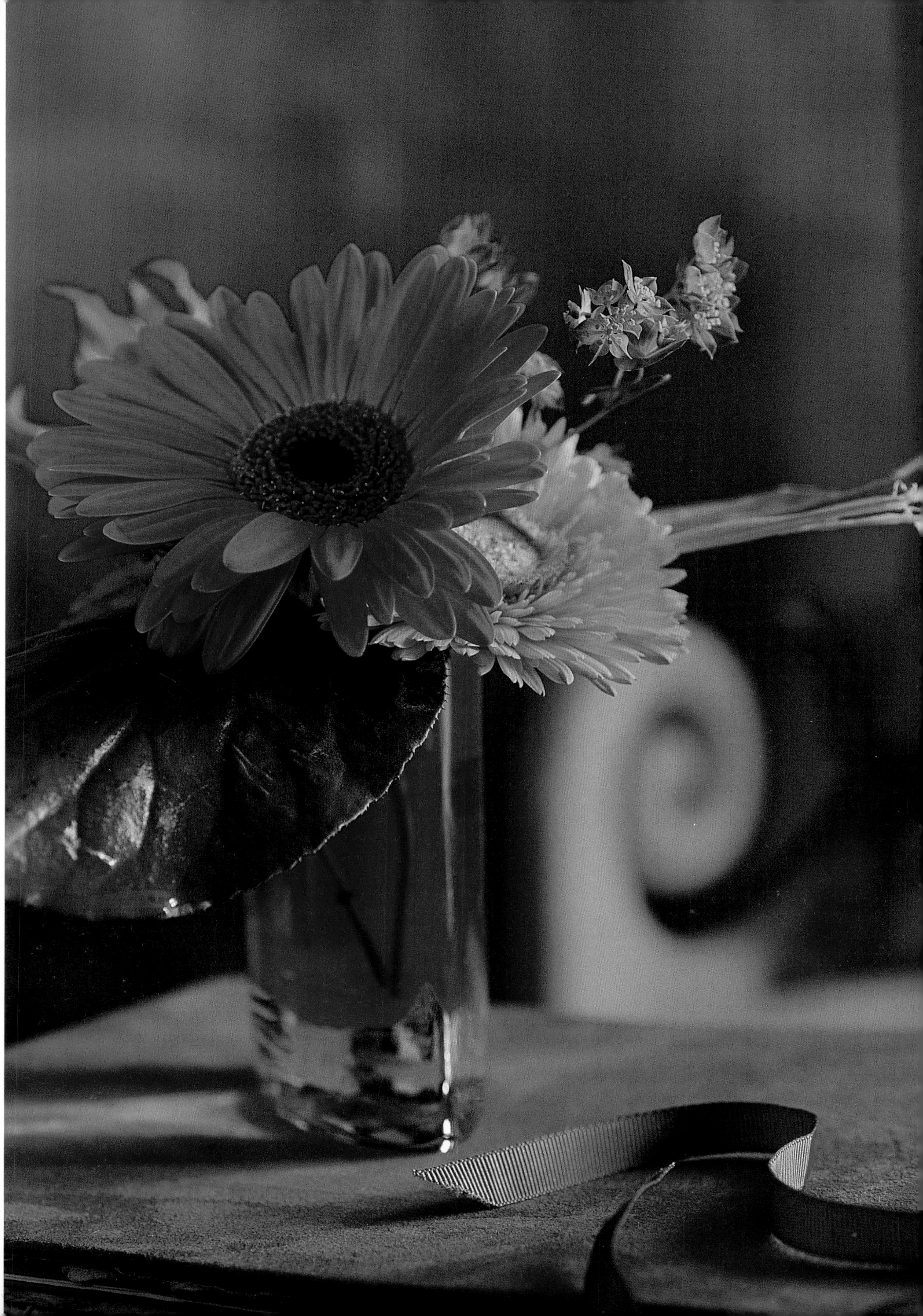

The modern city home is the ideal place to display contemporary arts and crafts. On the previous pages, a graphic metal fireplace and grate by Tom Dixon becomes a showcase for ceramics by Linda Hoffhines, while here, small multi-coloured pots by Henriette Gaillard are a microcosm of the rich colour scheme of the entire room. A snaky copper lamp echoes the curlicue arms of the Marouska Metz chair, while modern paintings sing out against the swirling abstract texture of the walls. The bright, vibrant palette embraces the colours of contemporary art but also of nature. Attention to detail does not mean making things fussy: flowers are simply and wittily arranged; cushions are trimmed with contrasting braid or simply sewn with string. Throughout the house, curtains are banners of natural sackcloth, frayed at the edges and simply embroidered; in this room, they are complemented by a single, asymmetrical drape in lime green crushed linen printed with gold.

At the other end of the sitting room, the introduction of orange and red to the colour scheme and the inclusion of a pair of curvy, overstuffed armchairs have created a comfortable, slightly less formal feel. Reflecting the rich cultural diversity of the modern city, the stripes of bright colour on a contemporary painted cupboard and handwoven rug hold a suggestion of India or Turkey, while at the same time appearing totally of the here and now. This is a place to sit and listen to music or read by the light of the French windows leading to the garden.

lime   raspberry   sapphire   turquoise

The city home often has to act as office, too. Off this end of the sitting room, a small, raspberry-pink study has been created, lined with shelves full of books. Bright colours and interesting textures, in everything from furniture to textiles and stationery, create a dynamic atmosphere. As warm and intense as those in a Howard Hodgkin painting, these colours have a strong emotional charge which is shot throughout the room, right down to the geometric patterns in the handwoven kilim. A turquoise ceramic-top desk by the window looks out onto the back garden, while small vases of flowers, or sometimes individual blooms, present the opportunity to contemplate nature at close hand.

WRITING
1991-93

On the garden floor,
former cellars and
servants' quarters have
been opened up, almost
to the limits of
structural feasibility, to
make an open-plan
kitchen, dining room
and small sitting room
leading onto the
garden. With its bank
of acid-etched zinc
cupboards and state-of-
the-art cooking
equipment, the kitchen
has echoes of a smart
urban coffee bar or
restaurant, but is
enlivened by bright fruit
and flowers and plastic
utensils and containers.

living

cooking

eating

bright

plastic

zinc

mosaic

café

shiny

At the other end of this floor, a bold contemporary mix of colour and pattern brings the dining and sitting areas alive, countered by the natural, neutral textures of driftwood, string-wrapped chairs and the pale stone floor. The stone continues through the wall of glass doors to the terrace and steps in the garden, an effective device that makes the room feel even bigger and blurs the distinction between indoors and out. For an informal lunch with friends, bright citrus colours, fresh flowers, hand-embroidered napkins and painted ceramics on a driftwood table echo the palette of the painting behind. Crockery is kept in the big painted armoire, its panelled doors picked out in two shades of turquoise. A bright magenta and orange checked sofa and shelves crammed with books bring an air of comfort and intimacy to the area of the room focused around the fireplace.

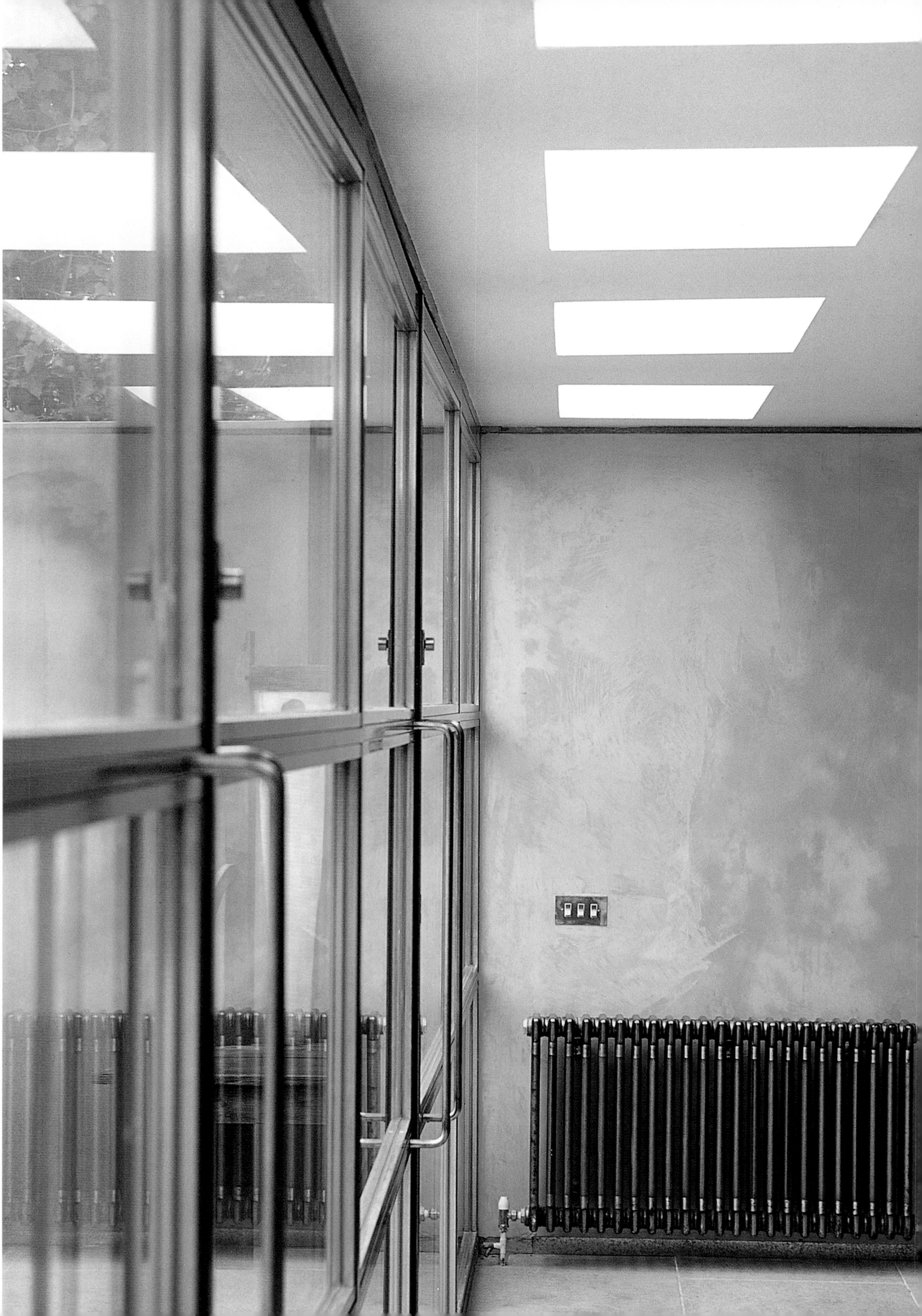

Along the back wall of the house, a bank of sliding glass doors and skylights brings in views of the garden and floods the whole of this floor with light. Centred around a ceramic fireplace by Ralph Levy, the sitting area is proof that it is possible to create an intimate area even in a very large space. In summer, the glass doors can be opened onto the pool and fountain outside, while in winter, the focus is inwards – the addition of a kilim in earth colours makes the space a place to curl up with a book in front of a log fire.

checks
stripes
skylight

The continuation of the same pale stone floor out through the glass doors assists in the illusion of bringing the outside in and extends the space of the dining room out to the garden. A square pool with a blue ceramic base and a simply designed fountain is reminiscent of the clean lines and pure colour of a modern painting; kidney-shaped stools and square pots of clipped box and helxine continue the theme.

Modern nature

Living in the city needn't mean losing contact with nature. The rhythm of the seasons may be less obvious than in the country, but it has its impact on our busy lives just the same. The urban garden or terrace is an opportunity to be free with nature: leave cottage gardens to the country where they belong and experiment with strong shapes and modern ideas. Urban inspiration is all around us, from smart new city parks in Paris and Barcelona to the quirky individuality of painted pots spilling over from balconies or hung from the walls of a secret courtyard, half-glimpsed from the street. Inside the house, reflecting seasonal changes in the way a home is planned and used can add a richness to city life and help connect us to nature and the earth. At Tricia Guild's house in summer, long evenings spill out into the garden after work – doors and windows are thrown wide open, curtains are minimal and the spaces are open and airy. When winter closes in, real fires are lit, dividing doors are closed for cosiness and curtains have another layer added for warmth and privacy. Throughout the year, the house is full of flowers – just a single bloom from the garden against a contrasting wall can have as much impact as a painting, and fresh fruit and vegetables from the local market are displayed in bright bowls or on open shelves. Wherever you live, the colours of nature are a feast for the soul.

'I am strongly attracted to the stimulation of the city — its architecture, parks and culture, the business life and street life, the theatre, museums and markets, the extraordinary mixture of people all gathered together ... the cityscape is just as inspiring as the countryside, but is more dynamic and individual ...'
Tricia Guild

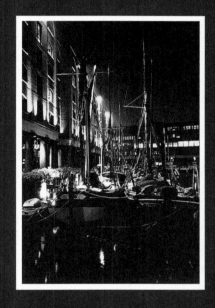

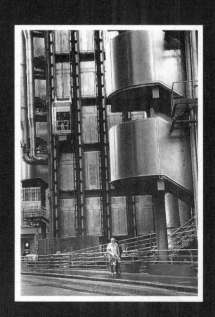

Arts and crafts

Cities are melting pots for cultures from all over the world, and the urban home is the ideal place in which to display contemporary arts and crafts. Loosen the definitions of what is 'art' and what is 'craft' with glorious glazed ceramics jewel-bright against a contrasting wall, a one-off fireplace in ceramic or zinc, bright handwoven rugs and other textiles. Hand-crafted objects have real soul appeal: their irregular, organic shapes and textures can raise the energy of a room, even adding something of the romance and ritual of cultures that are quite different from our own.

'In my view, "modern" doesn't have to mean cold and austere ...' I've tried to create a pure, almost minimalist framework and then give it an individual personality using shape, vibrant colour, exciting textures and the organic, quirky qualities of contemporary arts and crafts ...'
Tricia Guild

Tricia Guild has always been passionate about modern arts and crafts. Here, she incorporates them into the very fabric of the house. Contemporary artists Tom Dixon and Ralph Levy were commissioned to design one-off fireplaces for the principal rooms; the graphic metal of Dixon's plays against the more elaborate existing ironwork of the house, while the heavily textured ceramic of Levy's work (he has also made several tables) marries well with the swirling abstract textures of the walls. In the master bathroom, a stone bath like some minimalist sarcophagus is glimpsed through sliding doors of etched glass, while at the other end of the room, a bright blue Levy fireplace establishes a more intimate mood. Freestanding furniture is almost sculptural in its appeal – the snaky silhouettes of Tom Dixon's raffia chairs, the curves and curlicues of Marouska Metz's armchairs; even the towel rails look as if they could be bulls' heads by Picasso.

Some pieces seem reminiscent of distant, half-remembered places – the rubbed-down layers of brightly painted cupboards somehow suggest India, the striped rugs Turkey, the low-slung wooden bench and rope bed some nameless Pacific island – while at the same time they appear totally of the here and now. Everywhere there are much-loved paintings and ceramics, carefully placed against a coloured wall, to catch the light from a window, or grouped with candles, a handmade book and fresh flowers.

'The London city, with all its houses, palaces, steam engines, cathedrals and huge immeasurable traffic and tumult, what is it but a Thought, but millions of Thoughts made into one – a huge, immeasurable Spirit of a Thought, embodied in brick, in iron, smoke, dust, Palaces, Parliaments, Hackney Coaches, Katherine Docks and the rest of it! Not a brick was made but some man had to think of the making of that brick ...'
Thomas Carlyle,
The Hero as Man of Letters, 1840

'An atmosphere can be warm, dynamic, intelligent
and eccentric without being retrospective.'
Tricia Guild

Design and detail

It is the details that give a city home soul and make it totally your own. Tricia Guild's approach is to pay great

attention to detail without ever becoming fussy. Materials reflect the character and contrasts of urban life.

Here, skirtings and architraves are of galvanized metal recessed into the wall – a strong modern take on the

traditional alternative but also extremely practical. Textiles vary from utilitarian sackcloth and calico to rich

gold-printed silk and embroidery. Cushions and throws make splashes of colour on beds and sofas, their

different fabrics, patterns, trims and embroideries linked in a web of bright colour and texture that becomes a

personal signature.

From the first-floor landing, lime green walls give way to the calm but warm blue of the bedroom, where an Indian-looking day bed, strung with natural rope, is heaped with cushions and contemporary textiles all in shades of blue.

blue

natural

string

linen

calico

silk

cobalt hyacinth indigo azure sapphire sky

The bedroom's serene, all-encompassing blue colour scheme is studded with subtle, contrasting accents of pink, lilac and lime: jewel-bright anemones, handmade beads, handsewn blankets and a tiny, out-of-scale painting by Craigie Aitchison. There is a rich mix of fabrics: the curtains are plain white crushed linen, simply embroidered with string; on the bed, white and denim-blue linen and natural sackcloth are juxtaposed with a contemporary kilim and gold-printed silk throws. Again, the attention to detail is light and simple, rather than fussy and overdone. This sensual, nurturing space takes up most of the first floor, opening at one end onto dressing rooms to the right of the window and, through sandblasted glass sliding doors, to an airy modern bathroom at the other end. Running across the entire width of the room, the glass doors provide a degree of privacy while also enabling the bathing area to remain warmer than the bedroom; at certain times of the day the blue-green light that filters through them gives the room a dream-like, almost underwater feel.

Their walls painted the same zingy lime as the plastered landing, the pair of dressing rooms prove that organisation needn't mean a loss of soul. Floor-to-ceiling rails, open shelves of industrial glass and sliding drawers keep everything hidden but perfectly to hand; shoes are in neatly labelled brown cardboard boxes, while smaller items are packed in fabric-covered files. Everything is full of the promise of a summer's evening in the city. A lilac silk throw lined with sackcloth and embroidered in string makes for an interesting meeting of textures.

stone

linen

cool

glass

texture

light

calm

The bathroom illustrates Tricia Guild's exciting contemporary mix of dynamic colour and natural, neutral textures. Ultra-urban, semi-industrial materials like etched glass and brushed chrome are countered by the organic qualities of stone and wood, then brought alive in a blaze of colour down at the far end, where a painted blue wall, a swirling ceramic fireplace and the rich, irregular shapes of contemporary arts and crafts create a more intimate atmosphere.

at the top of the house

Up on the top landing, panelled doors, board floors and mansard walls retain their original, attic feel – somehow reminiscent of an artist's garret in Paris. Bright stripes on the blue floorboards are as vibrant as a contemporary abstract painting; the effect was suggested by the layers of ancient paint revealed when stripping the stairs and is continued into the bedrooms in the paint effects around the fireplaces and on the simple wooden furniture. In keeping with the architecture on this floor, the furnishings in the smallest guest bedroom are simple: a painted table, an old armoire and a bleached wood chair seem to echo the textures of the walls, while beds and chairs are given stylish but minimal coverings.

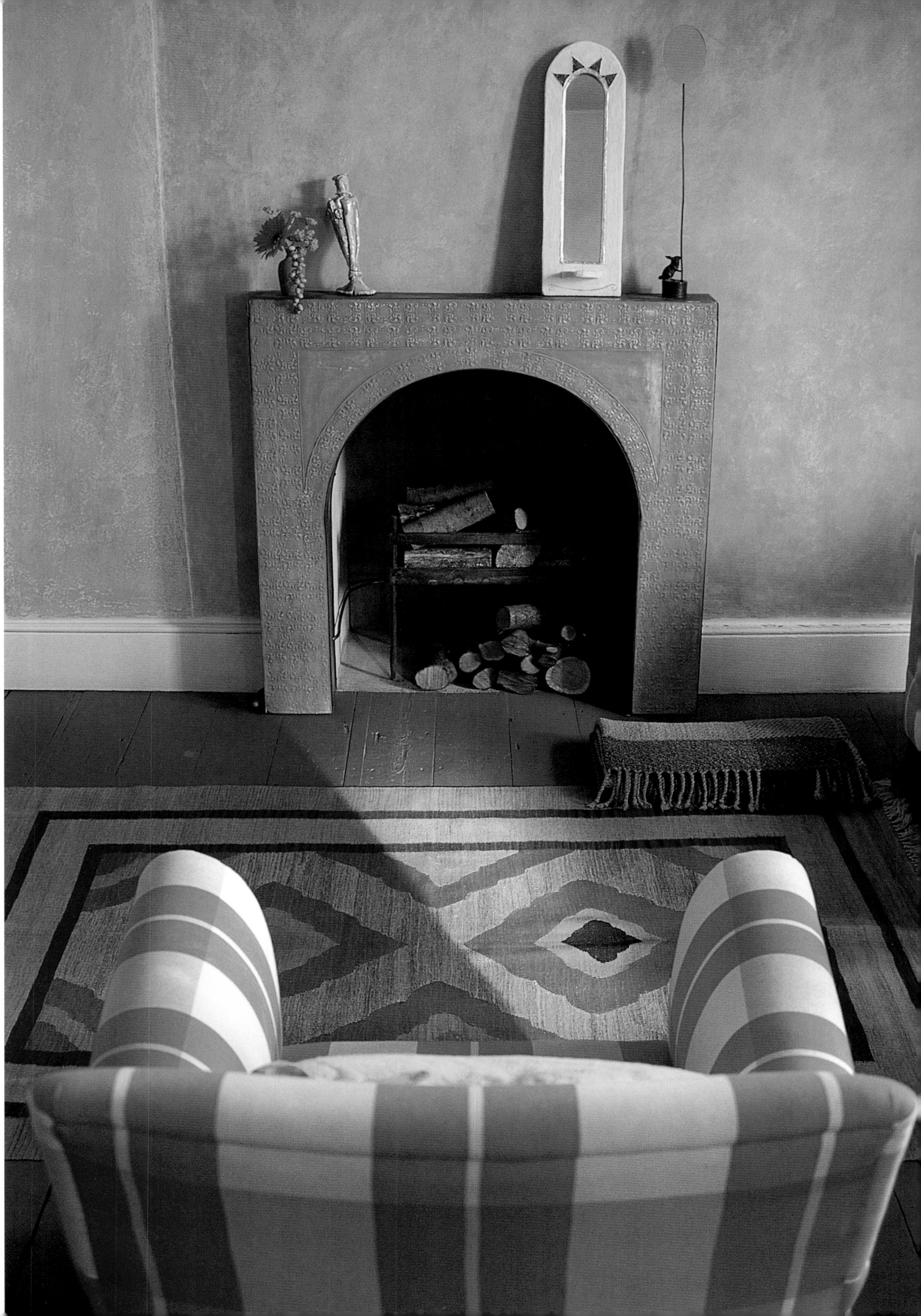

mandarin   peacock blue   magenta   citrus green

In the brightest of the spare bedrooms, asymmetrical stripes and planes of colour turn the walls into an abstract painting that glows orange in the late afternoon sun. A bold mix of patterns fills the room with energy: soft stripes, large checks, graphic flower prints and the geometric designs of a handwoven rug. Reds butt up against pinks; orange encounters crimson; acid green meets turquoise. The armchair in the foreground sums up the style: its traditional shape has been given a new, jaunty coat in a witty, oversized check, and it suddenly looks very contemporary. A bold tulip print on the bedcover echoes the strong turquoise ceramic fireplace, while accents of acid green make a stunning contrast against the smouldering sunlit walls.

The guest bathrooms are small and compact, simple without being spartan. Two walls are covered with jewel-bright mosaics; the fittings are plain polished steel. A sculptural towel rail, textured towels and fresh flowers in contrasting colours strike a more individualistic note.

lime

clean

light

fresh

stone

glass

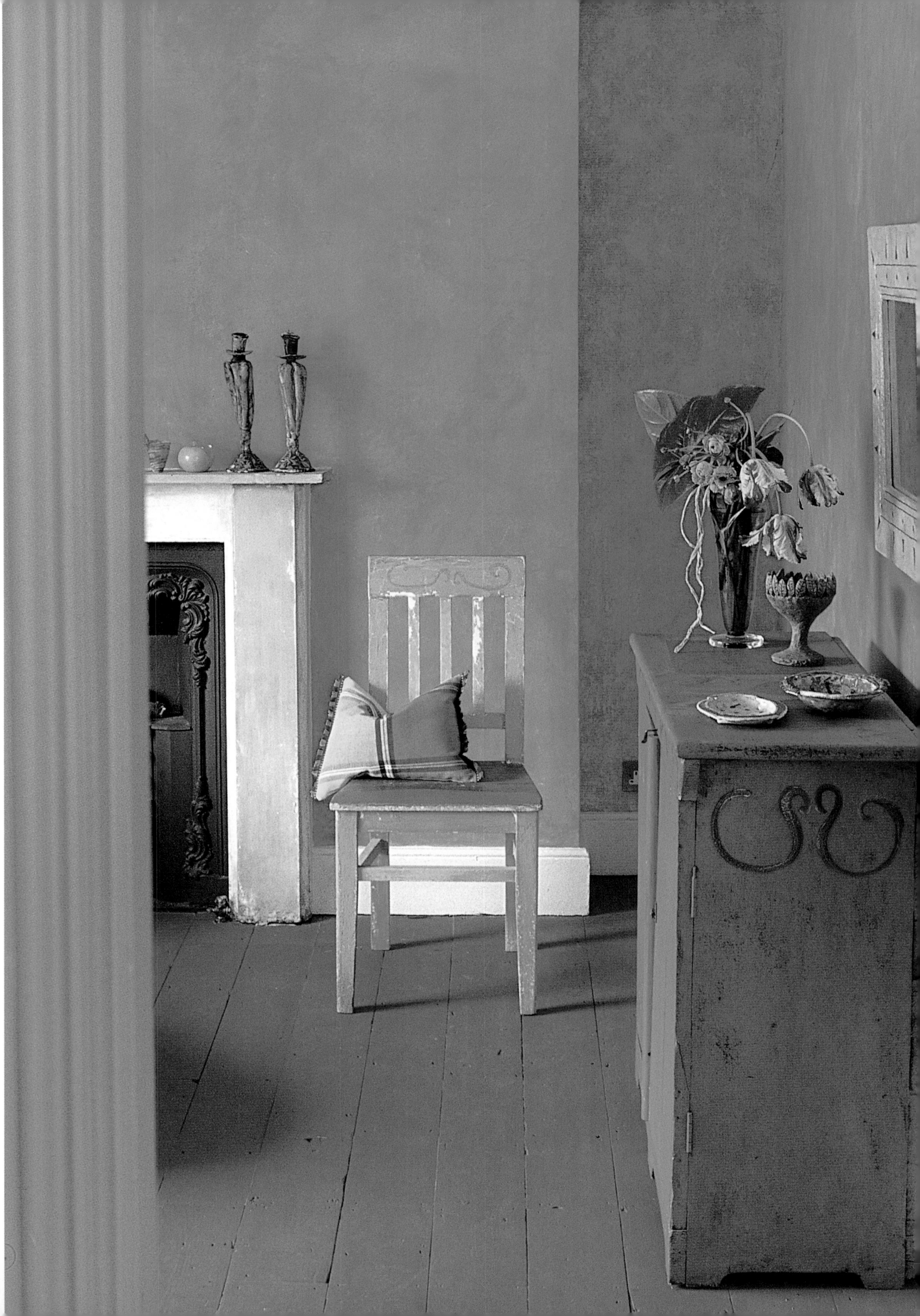

Blue floorboards and simple painted wooden furniture contribute to the breezy charm of this sunny top-floor sitting room. The aqua-green walls, rubbed and painted in soft hand-drawn stripes, have all the calm serenity of a Rothko canvas – one could gaze at them for hours. Small details prevent the style from slipping over into nostalgia: the crumpled lime linen cover on the chaise longue; the confident handpainted swirls on cupboards and chairs; a crazy leaning spiral metal lamp. Stunning frames and flower vases by contemporary artists and craftspeople sit on the simple fireplace, which is in full blaze every winter. The smallest guest bathroom has cobalt blue tiles – its main form of decoration – and semi-industrial fittings.

'There is great potential vitality in close-knit urban communities where social activity can be spontaneous and where the necessities and pleasures of life are close at hand ...'
Harvey Sherlock,
Cities are Good for Us, 1991

Urban virtues

Tricia Guild's approach to new urban living can provide inspiration for schemes in any of the rich variety of spaces the city offers as home. The houses and flats, loft and studio featured in the rest of this book all belong to people who share Tricia Guild's vision, and they illustrate the way in which exciting contemporary design can bring something of the spirit of the city into the way we live. The basic principles are adapted to suit each particular case – a clean, new space opened up as far as is feasible for a flexible way of life, the dynamic fusion of colour and texture, the rich contemporary mix of old and new, organic and industrial, arts and crafts. Similar ideas, materials and pieces of furniture crop up again and again, but each scheme is unique – appropriate to place, to a way of life and above all to personality – a distillation into physical form of an individual's response to the urban environment.

'In the dingiest streets of the metropolis are
to be found homes, the rooms of which are
lofty ... the ceilings beautifully ornamented,
the chimneypieces models for the sculptor ...'
Thomas Beames,
The Rookeries of London, 1850

Living histories

Cities are full of houses that were built for a way of life that no longer exists. Each one tells a story. The

Georgian crescents of Bath, the canalside burghers' houses in Amsterdam, the wedding-cake façades of Upper

East Side Manhattan may now form a part of the contemporary urban landscape but they bring something of

their history with them. Those who are susceptible to these things can sense this contribution in the ghostly

clatter of a horse and carriage pulling off into the night, the call of a street crier above the taxis, the shadowy

figures of girls dressing for a ball in the window of what is now a hotel. Even much humbler homes have a

part to play: the ridges of back-to-back cottages spilling down the hill from the (now disused) factory, the rows

of artisan's cottages where children once played in the street while mothers gossiped in doorways, the cobbled

mews – once stables for the rich houses behind them and later converted into studios by trendy Sixties

photographers. Only modern houses seem devoid of ghosts; but they, too, are products of their age, and their

time will come. Every house is a palimpsest to which we add our own layer of history. The challenge remains:

how to live in such places in a way which suits our contemporary way of life without denying the past?

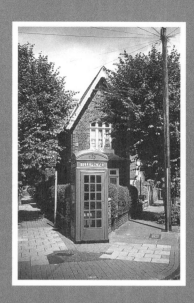

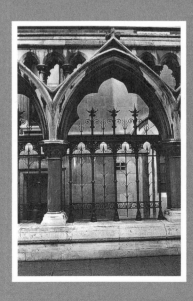

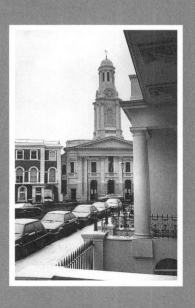

Easy modern living

One of the potential drawbacks of urban houses, particularly those built in the nineteenth century when most cities underwent rapid expansion, is that they can seem so similar: street upon street of Victorian bays or artisans' cottages, all with exactly the same layout inside. Given the chance and the money, modern architects can open up these spaces as never before – changes in lifestyle and methods of heating mean we need no longer rely on a network of small rooms focused around a fire, and advances in building technology offer the means. But even with a minimum of architectural alterations, quite ordinary houses can be revolutionised from within.

A major priority for most modern urban dwellers is an open-plan kitchen and dining area. Separate dining rooms are a relic from a former, more formal era of entertaining; nowadays the kitchen has become the hub of the house, where the modern working cook can prepare the food while chatting with guests over a glass of wine. An old dining room might become a nursery, study or TV room, while on the lower ground floor, former storage and servants' quarters can be transformed into an airy kitchen-diner. If the room opens onto the garden,

entertaining can spill outside in summer, with herbs and tomatoes, handy for cooking, grown in pots by the door .

Keep the decorations clean and contemporary; too many city kitchens try to emulate their country cousins. Raw, unfussy textures and materials rejoice in their urban roots: galvanised metal doors have all the no-nonsense functionalism of a French factory; the sheet-steel gleam of a semi-industrial stove calls to mind the best city restaurants; even the appliances can be streamlined classics from the roll-call of twentieth-century design. An underlying earthiness prevents such spaces becoming soulless. Pale limestone flooring and raw pink plaster walls form a natural, neutral backdrop against which the vibrant colours and organic forms of vegetables, flowers and plants fresh from the local market can sing out. Put some poetry into the details: in the crumbly texture of handthrown earthenware pots, or in sackcloth strips, sewn with household string, to hang up at windows or cover dining chairs.

Industrial meets organic

You don't have to buy expensive modern furniture to create a smart, contemporary interior. Just like people, even quite traditional chairs and sofas can be dressed up in jewel-bright linens, exotic swirls or candy stripes that will sing out in style against a contrasting wall. An adventurous mix of patterned textiles can bring a house alive with all the variety and immediacy of a streetmarket stall: stripes jostle with checks, swirls with curlicues, a geometric rug is placed at the foot of a sofa covered in wide bands of yellow, blue and green. Again, the secret lies in the use of countering neutrals to provide space in which the connections between the different elements can dance. Working with pattern is like composing a melody: themes must be repeated and picked up elsewhere if the effect is not to be chaos and confusion. Choose flowers whose colours echo the stripes on a sofa; pick out the principal tones in a painting; place plain cushions amid all the pattern to bring in the colours of the hallway or the room beyond.

Slow down the pace in the bedrooms and bathrooms; these are places to start and end the day with a calm clarity of mind. The same colour scheme can link the master bedroom, dressing room and bathroom – pale and restful colours such as powdery blue are good for sleeping quarters, but choose tones that are too clear and pure to be insipid pastels. All should be clean and simple, enlivened by contrasting accents of bright yellow, pink or lime. Windows can be simply treated, with silk plaid curtains tied to metal poles, crushed linen undercurtains or simple roman blinds. A sparsely furnished bathroom, pure white with accents of coordinating blue, and a cupboard-lined dressing room, empty but for a slip-covered armchair, provide the perfect calm environment in which to dress up for a night out on the town and to wind down afterwards.

Contemporary

'The city [consists of] relationships between the measurements of its space and the events of its past: ... the height of that railing and the leap of the adulterer who climbed over it at dawn; the tilt of a guttering and a cat's progress along it as he slips into the same window ...'
Italo Calvino,
Invisible Cities, 1972

pattern

The family town house
Strong modern colour in a period London home

Injecting some of the colour and immediacy of the city into this traditional Victorian family house has saved it from staidness and given it a jaunty, unconventional spirit all its own. Major architectural alterations were confined to the garden floor, where former servants' quarters have been opened up to create an airy open-plan kitchen and dining room where this young family can meet and eat; the rest has been achieved through a dynamic and adventurous approach to colour, texture and pattern. Familiar rooms are made modern with a coat of vibrant, unexpected colour; a traditional hallway is decked out in raspberry pink; armchairs and plump furniture are dressed up in exotic swirls and candy stripes. Even quite conventional objects such as mirrors and picture frames are given a quirky, contemporary twist.

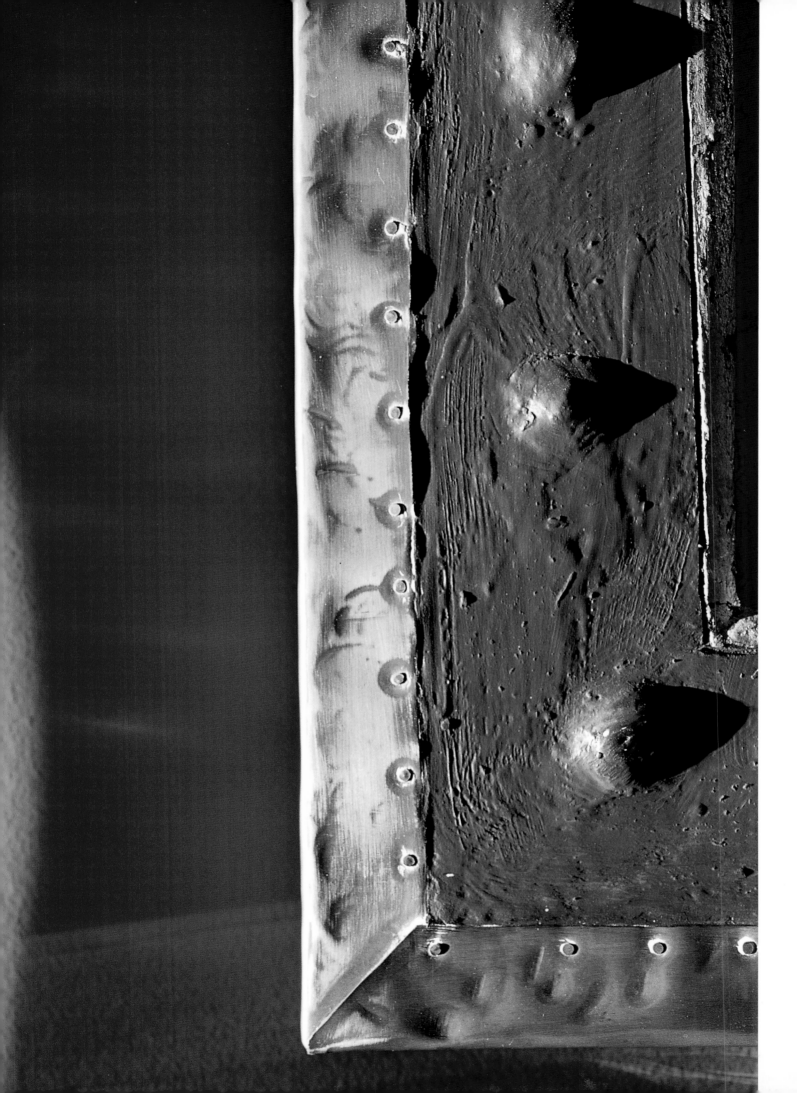

Bright modern colour, rather than any major structural reorganisation, has given this period family house a bold new look that is totally urban and contemporary. A Schiaparelli-pink hallway sets the scene and provides a contrasting frame for views into the rooms beyond — a lime green study at the rear and the rich cobalt blue sitting room, with its sherbet yellow and candy-striped furniture. In crisp contrast to all this contemporary colour, period details like the original moulded cornices, panelled doors and staircase balustrading are picked out in clean, bright white. With colours this strong, even the balancing neutrals can be more adventurous: coir matting a faded shade of indigo strikes exactly the right note of quiet interest, providing a foil for graphic mats and rugs and forming a modern take on the traditional runner on the stairs.

The adventurous modern mix of pattern in the sitting room is unified by sticking to a strict colour scheme, right down to cushions and ceramics, rugs and flowers. Stripes, swirls and geometric shapes; lime green, magenta, blue and bright yellow dance off each other to a rhythm that echoes the pace and richness of the city, from market fruit stalls to modern art galleries.

purple

yellow

cobalt

velvet

canvas

gold

Down on the garden floor, former box rooms and sculleries have been opened up to create a large airy kitchen/dining room, a small front sitting room for the nanny and children, and a tiny lavatory. A skylit extension with galvanised metal doors opening onto the garden creates an open, contemporary feel and brings the outdoors inside. This space is endlessly adaptable, moving with seamless ease from a family breakfast to a casual Sunday lunch, to an atmospheric venue for a formal dinner party. There is a modern, urban, semi-industrial feel about the sheet-steel surfaces and gleaming appliances; this is countered by the earthy textures of raw plaster, pale stone, terracotta, raffia, day lilies and freshly picked fennel.

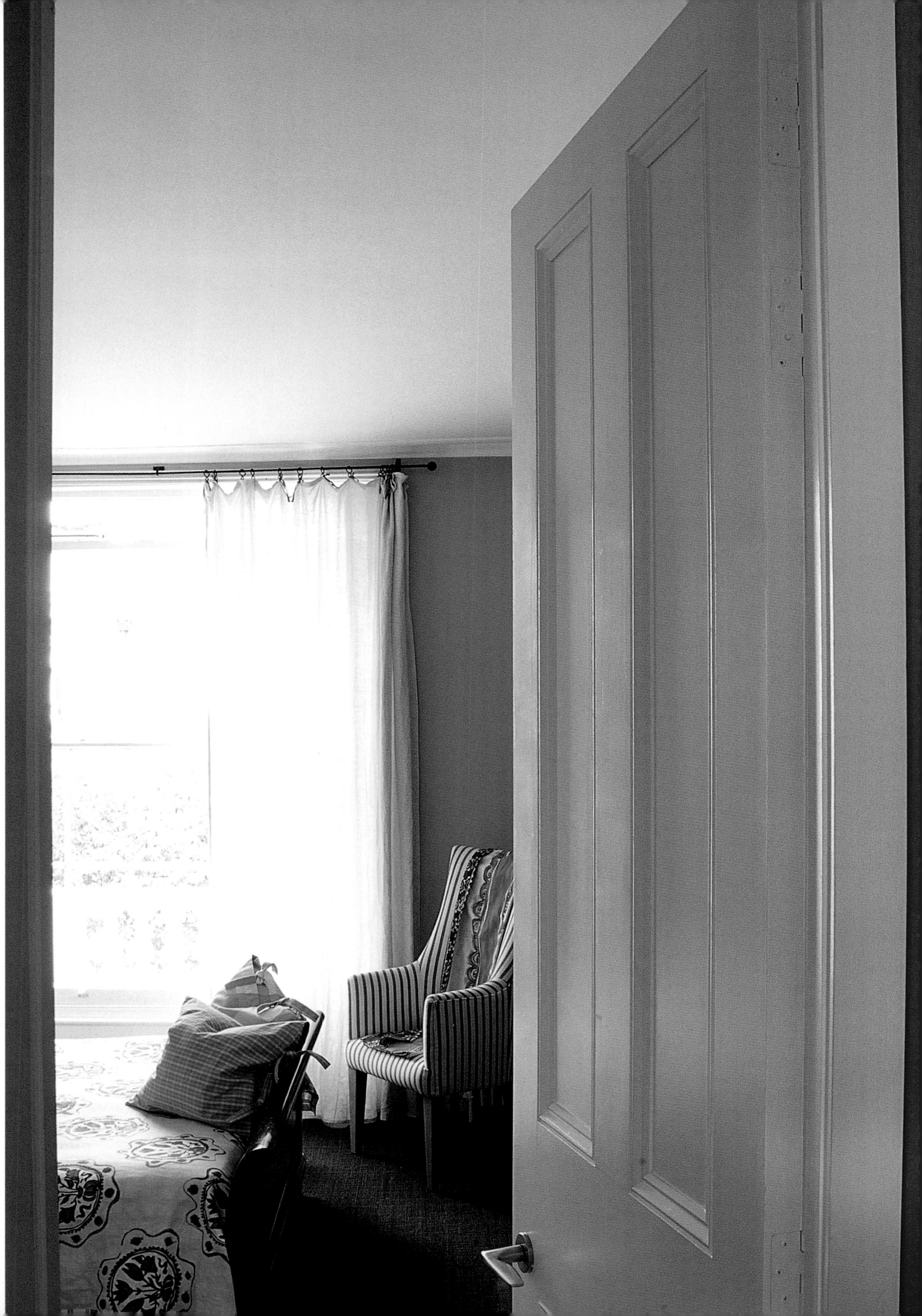

Simple and restful, a powdery blue-and-white colour scheme links the master bedroom and bathroom on the first floor. Crushed linen prints and contrasting silk checks at the window make for a modern mix of pattern; bedlinen is crisp white cotton appliquéed with indigo and cobalt. In a clever adaptation of the traditional fitted wardrobe, cupboards in blue-and-white painted tongue-and-grooving, with plain thumb-holes for handles, have all the shipshape ease and breezy charm of a seaside cabin; these are continued into the dressing room beyond.

simple

pure

bright

sky

white

A dressing room lined with cupboards keeps the bedroom free from clutter. This is the place where a night out on the town begins. The chair, like so many in the house, is a simple classic style dressed up in modern clothes; the pink linen slip cover and other accents of pink refer back to the central stairwell, the colourful core that binds the house together.

sky blue

cyclamen

mandarin

lilac

white

indigo

An artisan's cottage
A fresh mix of styles in a tiny mews house

Smaller mews houses and artisans' cottages, which still survive in many of the major cities of the world, make attractive and affordable first-time urban homes. Built as simple labourers' dwellings or, in the case of mews houses, as stables, they are as close as one gets to a country cottage in the city and, as such, are particularly prone to the lure of all that is rural. How to remain true to the place's urban roots without becoming dull and dreary? How to make such a house modern without denying its humble and very human origins? This tiny terraced house proves that a modern urban home doesn't have to be full of modern urban things; its artistic owners have crammed it with objects that have an old-fashioned, yet contemporary flavour, many of which they have found at street markets or on riverside walks. It is the unexpected uses and juxtapositions that keep the house on its cool, contemporary toes, and prevent it from slipping over into nostalgia. Textures are more important than associations: paintwork is intentionally crackled or rubbed back to reveal the underlying layers; an old table of ancient driftwood is given a runner of crumpled silk; an ornate paste frame, a fragment of moulded plaster and the pitted contours of a favourite fossil form an impromptu tableau on the bedroom mantelpiece.

The sitting room has been painted bright apple green to catch the early morning sun and form a uniform backdrop for paintings, sculptural fragments and other treasures. Sticking to a relatively strict palette is advisable in a small space like this: the dusty pink sofa looks good against the green, as does its complementary violet in the silk check throw and roman blinds. In keeping with the house's history, the furniture is honest and simple but given an arty, contemporary twist: tables are made from worn driftwood or spindly painted metal; threadbare armchairs have silk throws; cupboards are rubbed and crackled with layers of colour.

lime

violet

driftwood

washed

silk

cracked

crumpled

linen

The chalky blue bedroom and creamy white panelled bathroom are saved from countrified nostalgia by the interesting contemporary mix of materials and objects, many of which were picked up in street markets or on the banks of the nearby river. Shelves are made from curly metal or silvered driftwood; a brass bed is draped in a bold modern print; glass bottles, fossils and fragments of moulded plaster are arranged along the top of a fireplace. All the crazy contrasts of the modern city are here, but beautifully, and subtly displayed.

Space

The smaller the space, the greater the temptation to go down the retro-nostalgia path: counter this with exciting modern colour and an interesting mix of objects. Small urban houses often have no hall, the front door opening straight into the main sitting room. Confound the expectations of the traditional terraced exterior by painting this room a bright, unusual colour – yellowish-lime is good if the room catches the early morning sun, or go for cosy deeper tones for a space that is dark all day. There is often a lot of wood panelling in such houses which, if stripped or painted white, can easily smack of the country; similarly, architectural details such as picture rails or cornicing can look fussy and old-fashioned if picked out in contrasting paint, with the effect of making small rooms look even smaller. One solution is to give entire rooms a coat of matt colour that embraces all panelling, pipes, doorways, fire-surrounds and picture rails; the balancing neutral tones can be provided by the floor – either simple sanded boards or seagrass. The end result will be an illusion of space and a uniform backdrop against which paintings and other treasures can best be seen.

In keeping with the house's history, furniture should be simple and honest without ever seeming rustic. Spindly metal chairs and tables can be given a coat of unexpected colour; a threadbare armchair dressed up with a plaid silk throw. Wood and metal fit well here: wooden floorboards, chunky driftwood tables and fire surrounds, curly metal wall shelves, cast-iron grates and bold brass bedsteads and bathroom taps. An imaginative juxtaposition of objects and materials makes the mixture new and interesting.

Reinvention

Inspired by the weird and wonderful contrasts encountered on an everyday walk through the city, traditional objects may be given new uses and products of startlingly diverse origins can be brought together in new combinations. Like the remains of a building time forgot, fragments of moulded plaster become sculptural objects of beauty on the walls. Ornate picture frames are transformed into magical mirrors by the addition of old, foxed glass – kind to the eye and suggestive of ghosts. In the bathroom, a wedge of silvered driftwood from the Thames or the Seine becomes a shelf, a panel of cut crystal from an old pub makes an unusual cabinet. Play with the wit of objects used out of context: old folding garden chairs brought indoors or a turn-of-the-century railway clock. Everywhere the eye alights there can be food for the senses and fuel for the imagination. As in the world of the real city beyond the door, stories wait to be told, histories lurk under a veneer of modernity. A house can reinvent itself while not ignoring the hold of its past.

'A city is essentially a meeting of minds, and though we live in an age where these minds can telecommute, the street is still the most visible face of public interaction.'
Peter Jukes,
A Shout in the Street, 1990

'In the Paris of Louis-Philippe,
the bourgeois monarch, the
interior developed its
characteristic role in consumer
society as the realm of private
feeling, private wish fulfilment,
and private display of private
life. Décor might provide what
social revolution had failed
to deliver – the possibility of
each to realise his individual
utopia by populating his
own interior world with the
objects of his dreams ...'
Anthony Vidler,
The Scenes on the Street, 1978

Apartment life

By far the majority of urbanites live in apartments. This is partly due to pressures of space. Over the last hundred and fifty years of urbanisation, four out of five westerners and two-fifths of the world's six billion population have become city-dwellers; with land in short supply, an obvious solution to the problem of space has been to build skywards. Some experiments have been more successful than others. Places with a strong, longstanding urban tradition, such as France and Scotland, have developed models that are still inspiring today. The Parisian hôtel particulier with its well-proportioned, high-ceilinged rooms and matronly concierge remains an ideal model for urban living; and, for all its chequered history, the nineteenth-century Glaswegian tenement block, with its communal laundries and play areas arranged around a wide central staircase, is now being revived as a more sociable and humane alternative to the tower block. It is finally being realised that brutal sky-high boxes, where there is no common space for human interaction save a seedy and seldom-functioning lift, are not the answer, providing only a breeding ground for loneliness and crime.

Much of the history of a city can be gleaned from changes in attitudes towards its buildings and their different patterns of use. As the social make-up of cities has changed over this century, many larger residential houses in cities throughout the world have been converted into apartments, the majority of which are lived in by single people. Former churches, warehouses and disused office blocks are now being transformed for domestic use. There is a growing opinion that this is the way forward for our cities. Rather than expanding endlessly into the suburbs, encroaching on the countryside with even more low-density sprawl, why not work to re-inhabit the centres? Cities have always functioned best when their different components – homes and businesses, shops and entertainment – have coexisted side by side. Medium-density flats, either above shops, in converted

angles
lines
curves
geometry
symmetry
grid
circle

warehouses or in new low-rise blocks, can play an exciting part in the reclamation of the inner city. Living in a well-designed apartment can be the ideal way to enjoy a city. It can provide a personal pocket of space in the centre for less cost than a house in the suburbs, a convenient base from which to explore the excitement and facilities on the doorstep and a quiet retreat at the end of the day. For all the joys and stimulation of city living, home is also a haven in which to recuperate, either alone or in the company of a lover or a few close friends. Some city dwellers might set aside a special room, such as a peaceful bedroom on the quiet side of the building, a tranquil bathroom in which to soothe away cares, or a study for reading and undistracted thought. We all need a place to dream, where warm colours and talismanic treasures can transport us to imaginary worlds, leaving us refreshed and rejuvenated and ready to begin life anew.

'Whosoever leads a solitary life,
and yet now and then wants to
attach himself somewhere, ...
according to changes in the time
of day, the weather, the state of
business and the like ... he will not
be able to manage for long
without a window looking out
onto the street ...'
Franz Kafka, *Meditation*, 1913

Home as haven
The perfect urban hideaway

Of the city but one step removed, the ideal urban flat is a space from which to observe the life of the streets without getting caught up in it. Perched above London's lively Portobello Road market, these few rooms over a busy shopping street have been transformed into the perfect urban hideaway. Totally anonymous from the outside, its entrance an unmarked doorway on the corner of a parade of shops, the interior reveals a self-contained, private world. Rich in colour and sensual beauty, it is a warm red cocoon in which its young owner can forget the rest of life, forget who she is and lose herself in favourite music, books and paintings. The sunny roof terrace is a voyeur's paradise on which to sit, completely hidden from view, and enjoy a calm perspective on the hustle and bustle below.

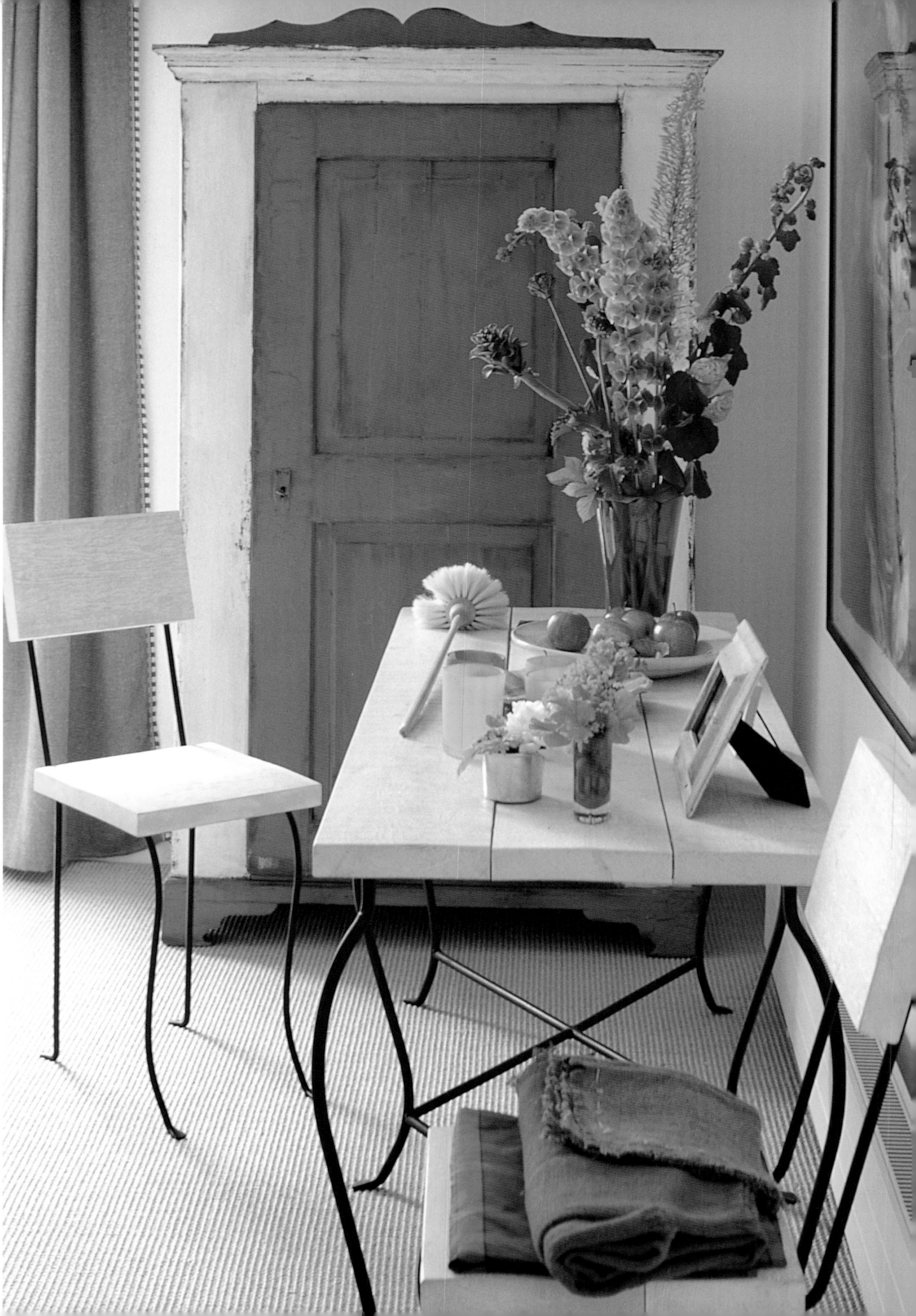

In the sitting room – by far the largest room in this tiny flat – white walls and upholstery, natural sisal flooring, sackcloth curtains and bleached wood have created a calm, neutral canvas that has been enriched and enlivened by accents of deep red and its complementary opposite, acid green. Favourite paintings are displayed on the walls or on the wide alcove shelves, which also provide a home for books and handpainted ceramics. One door leads into the diminutive kitchen, while French windows can be either thrown open to embrace the sunny roof garden and its views of the city roofscape beyond, or closed against the world.

bleached

wood

apricot

sunlight

thyme

mint

fennel

The vibrant colour scheme, countered by white and natural, continues into the bedroom where deep crimson and orange set a mood that is quietly sensual, nurturing and cocoon-like. Accessories keep to the same palette, from the bedlinen, a bold mix of checks, stripes and hand-appliquéed pattern, to abstract paintings, painted ceramics and a vase of overblown paeonies. Like the kitchen, the tiny bathroom is a feat of design: pale stone, bleached wood, sandblasted glass and plain white ceramic create a calm and soothing space in which to unwind or prepare for the day ahead.

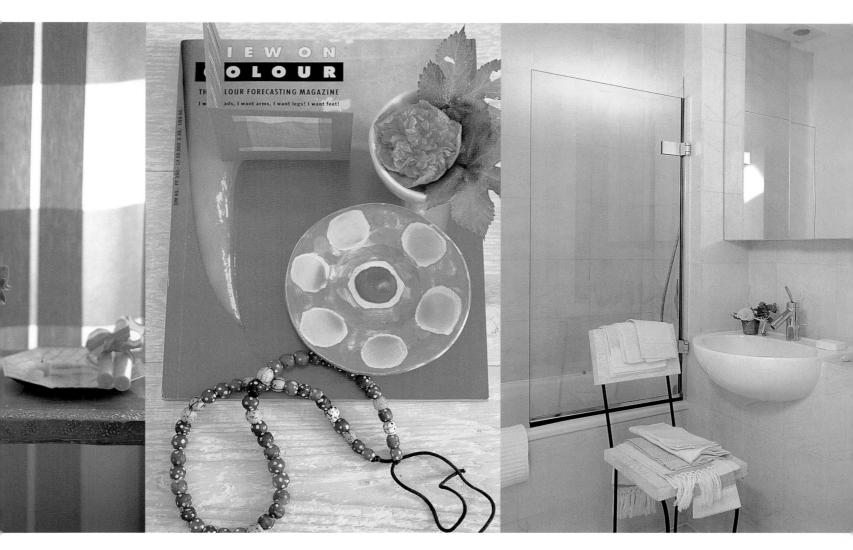

colour in a small space

A brownstone apartment
Contemporary arts and crafts in uptown Manhattan

Apartment blocks are a microcosm of the city itself: a high concentration of different people brought together in one place, all getting on with their own individual lives with varying degrees of contact and cooperation. For all their comfort and convenience, they can sometimes seem soulless places, but even the most anonymous space can be redeemed by bringing in something of the surrounding culture. The essence of a place is distilled into its arts and crafts, and the history of urban America can be traced in the beautiful handmade objects that have brought individuality and style to this collector's apartment in an uptown Manhattan brownstone. A pair of painted wooden masks seems to embody the brash excitement, urbane wit and ethnic diversity to be found in a city such as New York; hung at head height on a clear blue wall, they are powerful, provocative, pregnant with stories for the telling. Alongside objects that speak of the country's more immediate past, others tell a tale that is centuries old. Totem-pole imagery brings in the history of the Native Americans, while simple wooden furniture, reminiscent of the rural crafts of the Shakers, is given a witty twist as it adapts to life in the modern city.

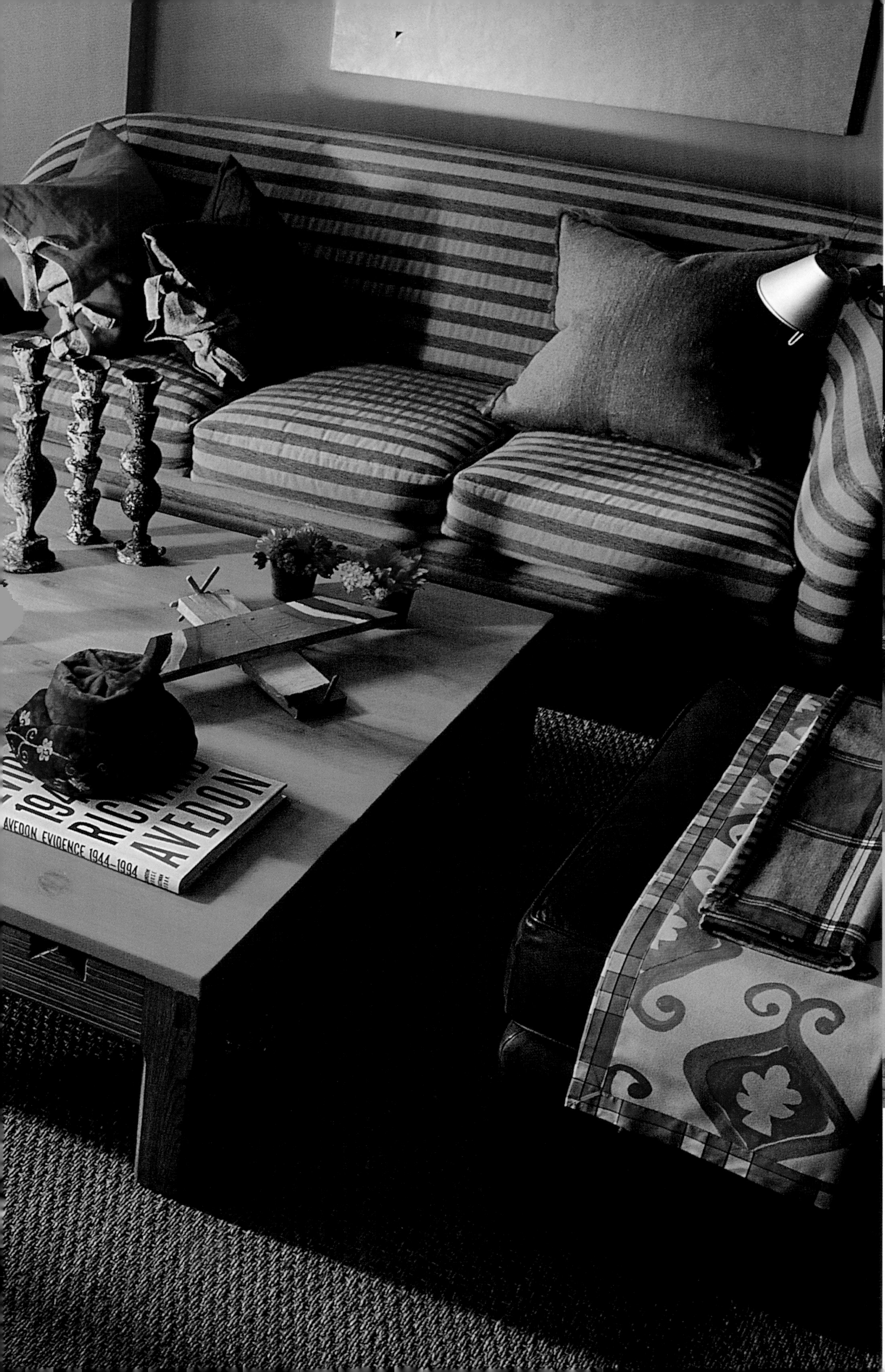
AVEDON
AVEDON EVIDENCE 1944–1994

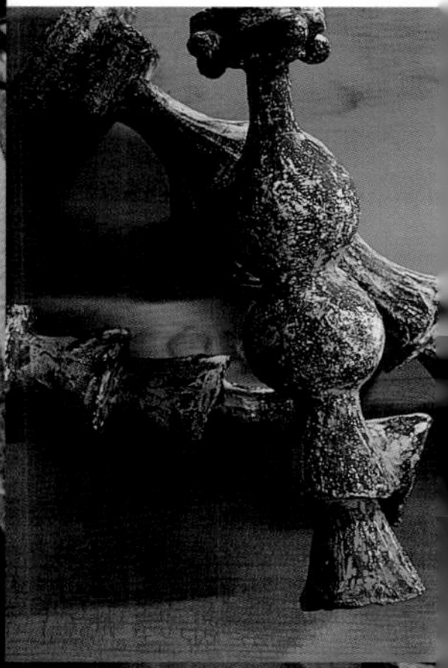

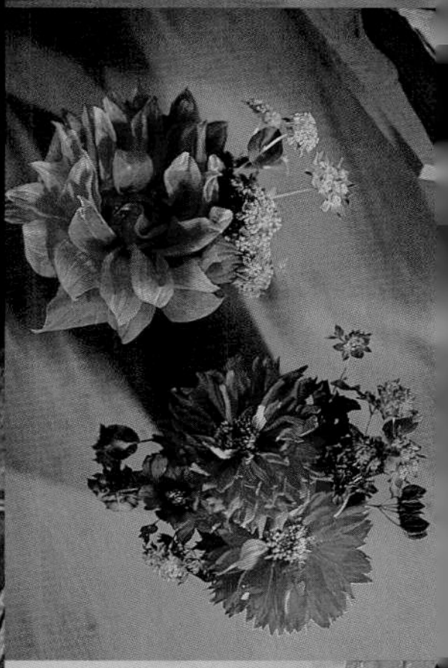

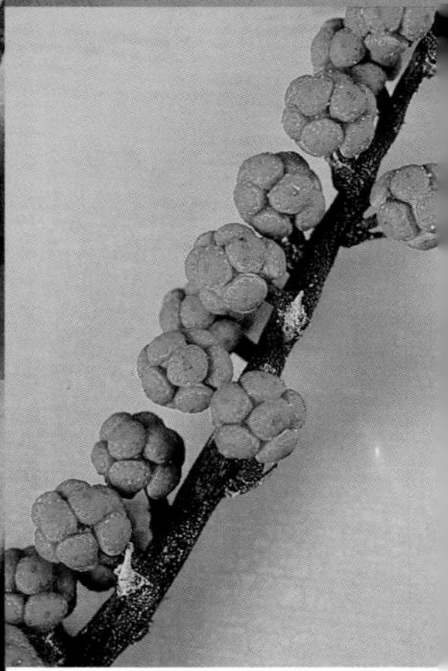

The terracotta and lime sitting/dining room is a dynamic backdrop for the fruits of the city: contemporary arts and crafts and fresh produce from the city farmers' market.

terracotta

turquoise

tomato

totem pole

shaker

In a small urban apartment such as this, so much time is spent in the main room that it is important to define the bedroom as a distinctly separate space. Here, the palette shifts to a warm yellow that seems to trap the rays of early morning sunshine as they filter through the blinds and printed crushed linen curtains. The mood is calmer, the mixture of colours and objects more restful to the eye and mind than in the rest of the apartment, though the carved and painted wreaths of fruit and John Derrian's découpage plates continue the harvest festival theme. Simple wooden furniture and handmade arts and crafts create a modern take on traditional Shaker style.

Planes of
contrasting colour,
painted furniture
and sculptures
made from wood
and newspaper
animate the
entrance hall and
connecting spaces.

'On any person who desires such queer prizes, New York will bestow the gift of loneliness and the gift of privacy ... for the residents of Manhattan are to a large extent strangers who have pulled up stakes somewhere and come to town seeking sanctuary ...'
EB White,
Here is New York, 1948

Living it up

New York has always had a strong urban tradition. Perhaps of all the world's cities it is the one that has held, and still holds, the strongest promise of fortunes to be made, dreams to be fulfilled and fun to be had. For this reason it also encapsulates one of the other principal urban traditions: a premium on space. As the modern skyscraper was born, the tiny island rose higher and higher out of the Hudson river in a physical manifestation of its inhabitants' collective hopes to touch the stars.

NYC, NY

From skyscraper towers to friendly brownstones, New York is the preserve of the apartment block. Invented to combine all the comfort and convenience of a hotel with the privacy and permanence of a domestic home, they fast became a metaphor for modern city living. To look up at one of these buildings in the evening, the windows lit up in bright rows, is to imagine so many parallel lives, so many stories, in many cases united only by the use of the same street door. Many city dwellers love the anonymity of such an existence, relishing their doorstep repartee with the caretaker and even the whine of the lifts and gurgle of communal plumbing at night. The major down-side is lack of character. The challenge, on taking on such a space, is to make it into a personal, emotionally rewarding home that goes some way towards reflecting both its owner's individual history and its wider cultural setting.

'The island of Manhattan is a gigantic metaphoric model of the compression of an immigrant ship that had moored and never left. Every apartment is like a berth. Every square metre of street is a deck. The sky-scraping offices are the bridge ...'
John Berger,
About Looking, 1980

Electric tension

It is unusual to be able to alter drastically the layout of a purpose-built apartment: in most cases the spaces are reasonably well-proportioned and sensibly arranged. Tiny galley kitchens are often a feature; if these can be linked to the main living space by means of a hatch or open counter top this may make for a more sociable arrangement. Even in a one-bedroom apartment, a large entrance hall may have room for a screened-off study area. By far the simplest way to claim such a space as your own is to make it a colourful modern display case for contemporary arts and crafts.

The higher up the apartment, the better the light, making it a good place to experiment with bold and unusual colour combinations. Think about using complementary colours, such as rich terracotta orange and turquoise, on adjoining walls, and savour the electric tension where the two planes meet. The other walls can be left white, on which accents of orange and blue can paint their own picture in the form of books and flowers, the stripe of an adjoining table top, the graphic brushstrokes of an abstract painting. Lime green for the sofa, a wooden table and other furnishings completes the three-point base of a balanced colour scheme, a rich autumnal palette that makes a dynamic background for a wealth of ornament, both natural and manmade.

'If you would be known, and not know,
vegetate in a village; if you would know,
and not be known, live in a city.'
Charles Caleb Colton, *Lacon*, 1820

Soul food

Too much arts and crafts in a small flat can make it resemble a gallery shop. The secret is to refine your collection down to the pieces that have a real reason to be there, both emotionally and aesthetically. Play with subtle references to your city's history and wider culture – Native American crafts and Shaker furniture in the United States, for instance; Moroccan or Breton influences in Paris. Bring in your own personal heritage, be it Irish or African or Eastern European. The modern approach to arts and crafts rejoices in the talents and values of different cultures, reflecting the social make-up of the city itself. Handcrafted objects have the most satisfying impact: a carved swag of fruit and vegetables or charmingly irregular pots and candlesticks bring their own idiosyncratic energies to bear on a room in a way that no mass-produced machine-made object ever can. They make the perfect complement for nature's own one-offs: overblown dahlia blooms, bowls of bulbous fruit,

crinkly edged cabbage leaves used as plates. Unify the scheme with a coherence of colour in these details, right down to curtain ties, cushion trims, the choice of crockery and glassware, and like a multi-stranded thread it will draw the whole together so it reads as food for the soul rather than confusion for the eye.

The same basic principles can be applied to apartments in house conversions. These can vary enormously, from the high-ceilinged *piano nobile* of a grand aristocratic residence to a small terraced cottage split into two. A few may be fortunate in retaining elegant proportions and attractive original features; the worst will have been carved up with more of an eye to economy than to quality of space. Again, the answer is to respond to the space available: clean it up, make it work as well as possible with a modern lifestyle, bring in some good strong colour and interesting objects. Be bold: if a place is lacking in character, this is the chance to create your own.

Old space, new space
A stylish stage set for urban entertaining

Theatrical colour and flair have made the top floor of a once-grand house in central London into a flexible space that can easily adapt to the hard-working, gregarious lifestyle of its stylish male owner. To maximise the light and illusion of space, the main room was painted white and accents of hot, almost Mexican colour added in the form of bright ceramics, striped rugs, potted cacti and painted furniture. Like a stage set, the space can be changed at the drop of a hat to fulfil a variety of functions: study, private sitting room or party venue. Clean, uncluttered and almost business-like by day, it can later be transformed, with the aid of an extra folding table, bright crockery, flowers and candles, into a magical, sociable setting for an impromptu dinner party. In summer, the windows are thrown open to bring in the dappled patterns of the London plane tree outside; in winter, an open fire throws crazy shadows across the walls and the mood is more cosy and intimate. The bedroom is flame orange, a striking contemporary setting for ethnic artefacts and the huge antique sleigh bed that holds the centre-stage.

textiles

mexican

leather

cactus

stripes

hot lime tangerine blue

The kitchen is decidedly unfitted: crockery and provisions are kept in a large painted armoire or displayed on the open shelves. One wall has been painted hot lime, a contrasting backdrop for brightly coloured paintings and furniture. Galvanized metal cupboard fronts, lamps and a miniature dustbin bring in some of the raw, semi-industrial feel of the city, while there is a cheerful individuality in the old-fashioned cooker and in the handpainted ceramics, vivid food packaging and fresh produce neatly arranged on the tiered blue shelves.

enamel   string   clay   zinc   ceramic

Fiery orange establishes a sensual mood for the bedroom, which is dominated by an antique wooden sleigh bed dressed in Egyptian cotton, raw orange silk and sackcloth throws. Talismanic objects sing out against the brightly coloured walls: Indian miniatures, an old foxed mirror, carved stone figures and other finds from abroad. Deep blue-green, the complementary opposite of orange, makes a striking contrast in the form of a painted wooden cupboard, its crackled and rubbed surface somehow suggesting India or Mexico. The dynamic mix of old and new, ethnic and indigenous, luxurious and utilitarian is endlessly enriching. Across the hallway, beyond the tiny bathroom, a small, private study is lined with books and files.

With its black-and-white tiled floor and sturdy, traditional fittings, this bathroom has a classically masculine atmosphere that is reminiscent of a smart metropolitan hotel. Simple, banner-style curtains in bold crimson and white add some strong colour, as do blue glass and bright towels.

Urban nomads

The city's population is always shifting and moving on. Few people, particularly the young, stay in one place for long; the average occupancy of an urban apartment is around two years. For this reason, living in one is often a case of making do with what you've got. Few people have the money or time to make extensive changes and, if the flat is rented, such work may be counter to the lease. This does not mean resigning yourself to a boring, impersonal box: you can claim the place as your own by means of your possessions and how you arrange them. Decorating a space like this becomes more like creating a stage set. Neutral or coloured walls provide different backcloths against which furniture and freestanding sculpture and plants can perform. The stars of the show are your personal objects: one-off or unusual painted furniture, paintings, ceramics and plants. Rather than spending time and money on built-in storage, let large painted armoires hide everything from books and files to hi-fi and clothes. In the kitchen, use galvanised metal to cover the doors of existing fitted cupboards and allow handcrafted ceramics, attractive foodstuffs and fresh fruit and vegetables to create their own decoration on open shelves. The less fitted your furniture, the more you can take with you when you go. Like actors in a play, when their part is finished, they can walk off with you to find new roles elsewhere.

'We should be reinvesting in the idea of dense and socially diverse cities ... shaping cities into compact forms and focusing communities around lively neighbourhoods ...'
Richard Rogers,
The Reith Lectures, 1995

One-room living

One well-proportioned space in an exciting location makes a better foundation for modern urban living than a rabbit warren of small rooms elsewhere. From tiny rooftop studios above elegant city squares to cavernous lofts in an old canalside factory, some of the most interesting urban homes consist of little more than one large room. Whether large or small, it will have to adapt to a variety of different functions: sitting room, study or work-place, venue for entertaining. The kitchen may be hardly more than a counter top and, unless there is a mezzanine or separate bedroom, the space may also have to incorporate a sleeping area. For such a room to feel cosy and nurturing when you are home alone but also accommodate lunch for twenty requires a degree of ingenuity.

Well-chosen wall and floor coverings can help define different areas. This might mean no more than mosaic tiles behind the counter-kitchen, a patterned rug beneath the dining table or a length of embroidered textile on a wall. Furniture may have to fulfil more than one function: a sofa may fold out into a bed, a cluttered desk by day becomes a dining table by night. Two matching tables can be united to make a large one and a stash of folding chairs kept in a cupboard is always useful, as are stools that double up as small tables. Armchairs can be focused around the fire on an intimate wintry evening or pushed against the wall to make space for a crowd of people at a party.

'It is not given to everyone to bathe in the multitude: to enjoy the crowd is an art ...'
Charles Baudelaire,
Petits Poèmes en Prose, 1861-2

Endless adaptability

The city is a great place for impromptu entertaining. Unlike in the country, where far-flung friends must be invited well in advance, fellow urbanites can drop by after work, or come in for supper after a night at the theatre or cinema. Spontaneity is part of the rhythm of the city.

When so much time is spent in one room, it is important to make the sleeping area a refreshing contrast. If it is a separate space, give it a completely different colour scheme and, in contrast to the activity and stimulation of the main area, keep it calm and uncluttered. If it is part of the main space, mark it off with moveable screens, or establish the mood with an embroidered bedspread, a handmade candlestick and a few particular treasures on the bedside table.

Open space

For many people, especially young and artistic types, the loft – a large, open-plan conversion in a former light-industrial building – represents the ultimate urban home. Infinitely more spacious than most conventional apartments, a loft offers a central location, a high degree of flexibility and fashionable, gritty, inner-city charm. Those whose hearts are in the country could never be happy in a loft. The phenomenon began in downtown New York, when artists and photographers set up homes in near-derelict factories and warehouses in the Sixties and Seventies. In the past two or three years, as the worldwide recession has rendered more and more inner-city office and industrial buildings available at affordable prices, the practice has spread to Europe and is currently taking London by storm.

Most loft spaces are sold as unfitted shells of around two thousand square feet, with plumbing for a kitchen and separate bathroom. The best retain some of their former industrial character in the form of steel girders, bare bricks and old metal fire escapes. But what do you do with all that space once it's yours? How do you define areas of different use without the conventions of doorways and walls? It has not been unknown for latterday loft dwellers, once the excitement of open-plan living has palled, to revert to convention, installing so many walls and dividing devices that they would have been better off buying a house.

Living in a loft is essentially one-room living on an enormous scale. Making a floor of an old factory feel like home takes practice and a degree of trial and error. Again, the theatrical, stage-set approach can be effective. To a certain extent, furniture has to define the space, so make sure it's large and bold enough in style to do the job; small-scale pieces and fiddly antiques will look like dolls'-house furniture at sea. As changing things around is part of the point, fit legs with castors for ease of movement. Wall and floor treatments can also suggest different 'rooms': one corner might have the plaster left raw to define the sleeping space, for instance, or the dining area a backdrop of pure, clear colour. Thoughtfully positioned rugs can also be used to mark the beginning of new areas. Where extra privacy is necessary, in the sleeping area, for instance, try making screens that are planes of pure colour on wheels; the 'rooms' thus formed can be expanded or contracted at will and the moveable 'walls' provide colourful backdrops for contemporary arts and crafts.

Room at the top

Mastery of space in a smart new London loft

In true urban tradition, the owner of the modern conversion flat featured previously has now upped sticks and moved to a fashionable new loft, bringing many of his familiar possessions with him. With its raftered ceilings, bare brick walls and fire-escape stairs, the seventeen-hundred-square-foot space bears witness to its former life as a nineteenth-century varnish factory, but has been transformed into a characterful and colourful modern home. Different materials have helped delineate areas of specific use: orange mosaic tiles form a backdrop to an industrial sheet-steel kitchen and glass bricks screen off the tiny, blue-tiled bathroom. The rest of the room can be re-arranged according to mood and function: its owner can relax after work with a drink in front of the open fire, or sit with friends around the dining table, enjoying the thrilling view across the rooftops. Two large new sofas and brightly striped rugs have helped define the different spaces, while simple coloured screens on wheels divide off the sleeping area and provide interchangeable backdrops for sculptural lamps and plants.

Steel girders, fire-escape stairs and bare brick walls mean this large new London loft retains something from its semi-industrial past, but the look has been softened by giving the wooden rafters a wash of white paint and bringing in some hot, vibrant colour. Large, bright sofas and boldly striped rugs articulate the main living space, while the kitchen is defined by a wall of mosaic tiles and the sleeping area by the blue 'wall on wheels'. Nature is not forgotten: mature plants have an almost sculptural appeal, the large cacti echoing the strong verticals of the girders. The double fire-escape doors, now painted a zingy acid yellow, can be thrown open for the ultimate urban view of the city skyline.

mosaic

peppers

marigold

hot red

shiny

metal

blue brick

orange

plastic

industrial

turquoise   zingy   tangerine   acid yellow

'I know of no other city in the world
where it is more agreeable to walk along
in a reverie than Paris ... How sweet it is
to take advantage of the present moment,
then to be lulled by the movement and
murmur of a city at once mad and
subdued, where the unforeseen has
always reigned supreme ... Paris wants to
live, it wants to live more than anything.'
George Sand

A studio in the eaves
Capturing the spirit of Paris in a rooftop pied-à-terre

In the busy late-twentieth century, many urban dwellers flit from city to city for work as well as pleasure. A small pied-à-terre, even one tiny room, is the ultimate alternative to a hotel, your own personal slice of the city in which to wind down after travelling and tap into your new surroundings. This rooftop studio in Saint Germain in Paris provides all the comfort and familiarity of a home from home for the professional couple who use it as an occasional base, sometimes together, sometimes alone. A fresh colour scheme, contemporary ceramics and a fine cotton check at the long casement windows let some of the breezy charm of the city blow in, and counter the idiosyncrasies of the ancient wooden rafters and shutters. The only clues to the precise location are in the tiny details, but the view from the windows could be of no other city.

aqua lemon ecru transparent gauze

As an occasional pied-à-terre, this one-room studio under the eaves has to feel instantly fresh and homely. In the daytime, the windows are thrown open to embrace the city below and let the breezy sunshine breathe life into the delicate turquoise, lime and yellow colour scheme. Breakfast is in the corner café, while lunch from the local *traiteur* can be eaten at a little table looking out across the rooftops. At night, when the shutters are closed and the candles lit, favourite ceramics by Henriette Gaillard and Harriet Thody, books and photographs, plus a vase of fresh flowers from the market in the square below, make this a cosy home from home.

This view through a casement window is reminiscent of a painting by Henri Matisse. Instantly recognisable, the Paris skyscape is framed by a fine cotton check that lifts and dances in the breeze. What better perch from which to enjoy a private view of this most elegant and artistic city?

'The City's voice itself is soft
like Solitude's.'
Percy Bysshe Shelley,
*Stanzas Written in Dejection,
near Naples,* 1818

Solitude in the city

Old cities like Paris and London have interesting nooks and crannies that provide for lives that do not fit conventional patterns. Even the smallest, most unpromising space under the eaves can be made into an occasional pied-à-terre or permanent one-person home. Through either necessity or choice, the majority of city dwellers live alone. French poets in their garrets, films like Hitchcock's *Rear Window* and the kooky apartments of Pedro Almodóvar's heroines all bear witness to a rich cultural tradition of solitary urban living. For some, it is true, the modern city can seem alienating and overpowering, and the prospect of living alone in its midst daunting and lonely. Others relish the peace and anonymity.

If you are lucky enough to have a small space of your own, a few friends and a modicum of good spirits, solitary city living can be a source of great joy. Living alone means taking care of yourself and your home should help you do this. Rather than a mere retreat from the pace of life outside, it should be a nurturing environment, planned with a view to meeting your own practical, emotional and spiritual needs. Choose your favourite colours and objects, and arrange the space so it feels intimate when you are alone but can still accommodate visitors. Take sensual pleasure in small things: the sunlight slanting in across the floorboards, a dish of peaches, a hand painted coffee mug. Have breakfast at the local café, lay a supper tray on the table by the window as evening fades over the rooftops. Then, shut the door and light the lamp.

Living cities

Cities have always been a focus for visions of the future. From Thomas More's vision of Utopia and the Bible's New Jerusalem to Le Corbusier's Radiant City, the New Town movement and beyond, the metaphor of the city has been woven into ideal political systems, new forms of architecture, blueprints for new patterns of human behaviour. Now, at the end of the twentieth century, our cities are at a turning point. We need to find a new way of living in them if they are to survive in their former splendour and if our all-too-precious countryside is not to be swallowed up by suburban sprawl. We need to fight the tyranny of the motor car, reverse the relentless compartmentalisation of residential, retail and business quarters, save the street market, the city park and the corner shop. More than anything, we need to create new living spaces that rejoice in the diversity of the urban environment and enable everyone to enjoy a modern, enriching and sustainable way of life. The time has come: cities are for living in again.

'The whole city is a park. The terraces stretch out over lawns and into groves. Low buildings of a horizontal kind lead the eye to the foliage of the trees. Here is the City with its crowds living in peace and pure air, where noise is smothered under the foliage of green trees ... Here, bathed in light, stands the modern city.'
Le Corbusier,
The City of Tomorrow, 1929

'Although cities are breeding environmental disaster, there is nothing in the nature of city living that makes this inevitable. On the contrary, I believe that cities can be transformed into the most environmentally balanced form of modern settlement ... In the beginning we built cities to overcome our environment. In the future we must build cities to nurture it.'
Richard Rogers,
The Reith Lectures, 1995

DESIGNERS GUILD stockists

The complete range of Designers Guild products is available through the Designers Guild Store at 267-277 Kings Road, London SW3 5EN. Designers Guild fabric, wallpaper, furniture, bed and bath collections are available nationwide including the following:

AVON

MICHAEL JEFFRIES DESIGN
3 Upper Lambridge Street
Larkhall Bath BA1 6RY
01225 310417

ROSSITERS OF BATH LTD
38-41 Broad Street
Bath BA1 5LP
01225 462227

BERKSHIRE
JACQUELINE INTERIORS
81 St Leonards Road
Windsor SL4 3BZ
01753 832549

BUCKINGHAMSHIRE
JOHN LEWIS FURNISHINGS
& LEISURE
Holmers Farm Way
Cressex Centre
High Wycombe HP12 4NW
01494 462666

MORGAN GILDER FURNISHINGS
83 High Street
Stony Stratford
Milton Keynes MK11 1AT
01908 568674

CAMBRIDGESHIRE
AT HOME
44 Newnham Road
Cambridge CB3 9EY
01223 321283

CHANNEL ISLANDS
THE DESIGNERS CHOICE
21 Seale Street
St Helier
Jersey JE2 3QG
01534 24678

F LE GALLAIS AND SONS
Bath Street St. Helier
Jersey JE1 1BR
01534 30202

CHESHIRE
DESIGNERS
15 London Road
Alderley Edge SK9 7UT
01625 586851

HAMILTON BROWN
2a Abbey Green
Chester CH1 2JH
01244 341116

MARGARET-ANNE INTERIORS
121 King Street
Knutsford WA16 6EH
01565 632178

ROSI INTERIORS
22 Victoria Road
Hale WA15 9AD
0161 929 9780

DEVON
G & H INTERIORS
1 The Old Pannier Market
High Street
Honiton EX14 8LS
01404 42063

DORSET
INDIVIDUAL INTERIOR DESIGN
58-60 Poole Road
Westbourne
Bournemouth BH4 9DZ
01202 763256

EIRE
HELEN CASEY INTERIOR DESIGN
No 4 Clonmore Villas Tralee
066 24216

COTTON BOX INTERIORS
21 Middle Street Galway
091 564373

J. LYONS INTERIORS
The Square Castlerea
Co Roscommon
0907 20339

ESSEX
CLEMENT JOSCELYNE
9-11 High Street
Brentwood CM14 4RG
01277 225420

DEVON HOUSE INTERIORS
3-4 Devon House
Hermon Hill Wanstead
Essex E11 2AW
0181 518 8112

GLOUCESTERSHIRE
UPSTAIRS DOWNSTAIRS
19 Rotunda Terrace
Montpellier Street
Cheltenham GL50 1SW
01242 514023

HAMPSHIRE
CONCEPT INTERIORS
The Ivy House 1 Folly Lane
Petersfield
Hants GU31 4AU
01730 233 633

INTERIOR DESIGN WORKSHOP
Studio 3
20a Jewry Street Winchester
Hants SO23 8RZ
01962 855 763

PAT STAPLES INTERIORS
Symes Corner
1 Houchin Street
Bishop's Waltham SO3 1AR
01489 892626

THE INTERIOR TRADING
COMPANY
57 Marmion Road
Southsea PO5 2AT
01705 838 038

**HEREFORDSHIRE &
WORCESTERSHIRE**
ALLAN VAUGHAN LTD
6 Bank Street
Link Top Malvern WR14 2JN
01684 892638

CLOUD NINE INTERIORS
12 St. Andrews Street
Droitwich
WR9 8DY
01905 779988

HERTFORDSHIRE
AMICUS FABRICS LTD
32 Bancroft
Hitchin SG5 1LA
01462 436989

BEVERLEY HILLS INTERIORS
214 High Street
Barnet EN5 5SZ
0181 441 8566

CLEMENT JOSCELYNE
Market Square
Bishop's Stortford
CM23 3XA
01279 506731

CLEMENT JOSCELYNE
111-112 Bancroft
Hitchin SG5 1LT
01462 436533

DAVID LISTER INTERIORS
6 Leydon Road
Harpenden AL5 2TL
01582 764270

HEATH HOUSE
72A High Road
Bushey Heath WD2 3JE
0181 950 3117

KENT
JOHN THORNTON INTERIORS
43 St Peter's Street
Canterbury CT1 2BG
01227 785284

KENT HOUSE SOFAS
206 Kent House Road
Beckenham BR3 1JN
0181 778 7782

KOTIKI INTERIORS
22-24 Grove Hill Road
Tunbridge Wells TN1 1RZ
01892 521369

MARY ENSOR INTERIORS
13 Crescent Road
Tunbridge Wells
TN1 2LU
01892 523003/511525

THOMAS TUBB INTERIORS
182 Petts Wood Road
Petts Wood BR5 1LG
01689 830853

LANCASHIRE
CAMPION
24 High Street
Uppermill
Saddleworth
Nr Oldham OL3 6HX
01457 876341

JOHN THOMPSON DESIGN
CENTRE
328-336 Church Street
Blackpool FY1 3QH
01253 302515

LEICESTERSHIRE
HARLEQUIN INTERIORS
11 Loseby Lane
Leicester LE1 5DR
0116 2620 994

ROOM SERVICE INTERIORS
3 Shambles Court Bell Street
Lutterworth LE17 4DW
01455 550304

LINCOLNSHIRE
PILGRIM DECOR
35 Wide Bargate
Boston PE21 6SR
01205 363917

LONDON
DESIGNERS GUILD STORE
267-277 Kings Road SW3 5EN
0171 351 5775

BELLEVUE INTERIORS
1 Bellevue Parade
Bellevue Road
Wandsworth Common
SW17 7EQ
0181 767 6659

CHEONG INTERIORS
86 Stoke Newington Church
Street N16 OAP
0171 923 7894

HARRODS
87-135 Brompton Road
Knightstbridge SW1X 7XL
0171 730 1234

HEAL & SON
196 Tottenham Court Road
W1P 9LD
0171 636 1666

JOHN LEWIS
Oxford Street W1A 1EX
0171 629 7711

PETER JONES
Sloane Square SW1W 8EL
0171 730 3434

INTERIORS OF CHISWICK
454-458 Chiswick High Road
W4 5TT
0181 994 0073

INTERMURA FURNISHINGS LTD
27 Chalk Farm Road NW1 8AG
0171 485 6638

LIBERTY
Regent Street W1 6AH
0171 734 1234

MILLPOND INTERIORS
4&6 West Lane SE16 4NY
0171 231 0700

MR JONES
175-179 Muswell Hill Broadway
Muswell Hill N10 3RS
0181 444 6066

PAINE AND CO
47-51 Barnsbury Street
Islington N1 1TP
0171 607 1176

PENNYBEE DESIGNED INTERIORS
53-54 High Street
Wimbledon Village SW19 5AX
0181 947 7224

SELFRIDGES
Oxford St W1A 1AB
0171 629 1234

TESSUTI CASA LIMITED
51A St John's Wood High Street
NW8 7NJ
0171 722 0977

GREATER MANCHESTER
HOMES UNLIMITED
2 Warburton Street
Didsbury Village
Manchester M20 6WA
0161 434 6278

POPPEE DESIGN LTD
Newbury House
403 Bury New Road
Salford M7 2BT
0161 792 4308

MIDDLESEX
HAMPTON INTERIORS LTD
169B High Street
Hampton Hill TW12 1NL
0181 979 8425

NORFOLK
CLEMENT JOSCELYNE
The Granary 5 Bedford Street
Norwich NR2 1AL
01603 623220

NORTHAMPTONSHIRE
CLASSIX DESIGN &
DEVELOPMENT LTD
The Old Trinity Church
245 Wellingborough Road
Northampton NN1 4EH
01604 232322

NORTHERN IRELAND
FULTONS FINE FURNISHINGS
Hawthorne House
Boucher Crescent
Belfast BT12 6HU
01232 382 168

The Point Derrychara
Enniskillen BT74 6JF
01365 323739

55-63 Queen Street
Lurgan BT66 8BN
01762 325768

NOTTINGHAMSHIRE
LILLIE INTERIORS
16 London Road
Newark NG24 1TW
01636 705693

NASH INTERIORS
17-19 Carlton Street
Nottingham NG1 1NL
01159 413891

OXFORDSHIRE
STELLA MANNERING LTD
2 Woodstock Road
Oxford OX2 6HT
01865 57196

SCOTLAND
ADAM McNEE INTERIOR
DESIGN LTD
75 Kinnoull Street
Perth PH1 5EZ
01738 636917

CAIRNS INTERIORS
111-113 High Street
Old Aberdeen AB2 3EN
01224 487490

DECOR (ABERDEEN)
157 Skene Street
Aberdeen AB1 1QL
01224 646533

DESIGNWORKS
38 Gibson Street
Glasgow G12 8NX
0141 339 9520

INSIDE STORY
The Meadows Auldearn
Nairn Shire Highland Region
IV12 5JZ
01667 453826

JOHN LEWIS
St James Centre
Edinburgh EH1 3SP
0131 556 9121

LINDA REID PLUS
188 Fenwick Road
Giffnock
Glasgow G46 6XF
0141 620 1299

MARY MAXWELL
63 Dublin St
Edinburgh EH3 6NS
0131 557 2173

SOMERSET
THE CURTAIN POLE
64 High Street
Glastonbury BA6 9DY
01458 834166

PAUL CARTER
The Studio
Elm House Chip Lane
Taunton TA1 1BZ
01823 330404

STAFFORDSHIRE
ANN CLARKE DESIGN
36 Tamworth Street
Lichfield WS13 6JJ
01543 416366

THE WILLIAM MORRIS SHOP
313 Hartshill Road
Hartshill
Stoke on Trent ST4 7NR
01782 619772

SUFFOLK
CLEMENT JOSCELYNE
16 Langton Place
Bury St Edmunds IP33 1NE
01284 753824

EDWARDS OF HADLEIGH
53 High Street
Hadleigh IP7 5AB
01473 827271

SURREY
HEAL & SON
Tunsgate
Guildford GU1 3QU
01483 576715

INTERIOR MOTIVES
151 Shirley Road
Croydon CRO 8SS
0181 654 2776

JOHN LEWIS
Wood Street
Kingston upon Thames
KT1 1TE
0181 547 3000

HOMEFLAIR
50 Coombe Road
Kingston upon Thames
KT2 7AF
0181 546 8921

INTERIOR OPTIONS
276 Ewell Road
Surbiton KT6 7AG
0181 399 9602

J DECOR INTERIORS
159-161 High Street
Epsom KT19 8EW
01372 721773

PIPELINE-IN-DEC
OF COBHAM
8 Postboys Row
Between Streets
Cobham KT11 1AB
01932 862764

SUSSEX
CARVILLS FURNISHINGS LTD
112-114 High Street
Uckfield
East Sussex TN22 1PX
01825 763456

ENGLISH INTERIORS
Haywards Heath Road
Balcombe
West Sussex RH17 6PE
01444 811700

SUTTONS OF EAST GRINSTEAD
25-27 High Street
East Grinstead RH19 3AF
01342 321695

THE DESIGN HOUSE
56A High Street
Steyning
West Sussex BN44 3RD
01903 812845

TYNE AND WEAR
ABERCROMBIES
142 Manor House Road
Jesmond
Newcastle upon Tyne
NE2 2NA
0191 281 7182

ROY ERRINGTON (WB) LTD
6 Cauldwell Lane
Monkseaton
Whitley Bay NE25 8LN
0191 252 7316

WINDOWS AND WALLS
7 Station Road Fulwell
Sunderland SR6 9AA
0191 548 1414

WALES
COUNTRY INTERIORS
Goat Street
Haverfordwest
Dyfed SA61 1PX
01437 768217

MASKREYS
116-120 Whitchurch Road
Cardiff CF4 3YL
01222 229371

RENOIR INTERIORS
28 St Helens Road
Swansea SA1 4AP
01792 648513

WARWICKSHIRE
COLESHILL INTERIORS AND
ANTIQUES
12-14 High Street
Coleshill B46 1AZ
01675 467416

WEST MIDLANDS
BENNETT AND BOWMAN
INTERIORS LTD
4 Beeches Walk
Sutton Coldfield B73 6HN
0121 354 9371

HOGARTH INTERIORS
Winwood Court
Norton Road
Stourbridge DY8 2AE
01384 444664

JAS INTERIOR DESIGN
CONSULTANTS
281 Tettenhall
Newbridge
Wolverhampton WV6 OLE
01902 744441

JOHN CHARLES INTERIORS
349 Hagley Road
Edgbaston
Birmingham B17 8DN
0121 420 3977

MOONLIGHT STUDIOS LTD
248 Lyndon Road
Olton
Solihull B92 7QW
0121 7436613

YORKSHIRE

HOMEWORKS
4 Castlegate
Tickhill
Doncaster DN11 9QU
01302 743978

MADELAINE PEACE INTERIORS
145 Oakbrook Road
Sheffield S11 7EB
0114 2306666

MARTIN STUART
292-294 Abbeydale Road
Sheffield S7 1FL
0114 258 2462

PLASKITT & PLASKITT
8A Walmgate
York YO1 2TJ
01904 624670

SUE RUGG SOFT FURNISHING
DESIGN SPECIALIST
11 Eastgate Bramhope
Leeds LS16 9AT
01532 842960
Scarborough
01723 352198

Designers Guild fabrics and
wallpapers are also available
from all John Lewis Partnership
Department Stores

Designers Guild products are
available in over 40 countries
including the following:

ARGENTINA
MRS MIRANDA GREEN
Cabello 3919
1425 Buenos Aires
Tel: (00 54 1) 802 0850

AUSTRALIA
WARDLAW PTY LIMITED
230-232 Auburn Road
Hawthorn
3122 Melbourne Victoria
Tel: (00 61 3) 9 819 4233

AUSTRIA
VICTORIA SCHOELLER-SZ‹TS
Boersegasse 9 #10
A-1010 Wien
Tel: (00 43 1) 535 3075

BELGIUM & LUXEMBOURG
CARL SPRL
Avenue de l'Hippodrome 5
B-1050 Brussels
Tel: (00 32 2) 640 8570

BERMUDA
HOWE ENTERPRISING
Suite 375 48 Par-La-Ville Road
Hamilton HM 11
Tel: (00 1 809) 292 1433

BRAZIL
HUMBERTO
Escriotria Central Sao Paulo
R. Barata Ribeiro 263
Tel: (00 55 11) 257 3977

CANADA
PRIMAVERA
160 Pears Avenue Suite 210
Toronto M5R 1TA
Tel: (00 1 416) 921 3334

CHILE
ROOMS DECORACIONES LTD
Alonso de Cordova 3875-3
Vitacura Santiago
Tel: (00 56 2) 207 9150

COLOMBIA
DENISE WEBB AND ASSOCIATES
DISE – O INTERIOR
Calle 79B No. 7-85
Bogotà Colombia
Tel: (00 571) 217 1441

CYPRUS
L. I. CHRISTOFIDES
P O Box 1310
9 Loukis Akritas Ave Nicosia
Tel: (00 357 2) 462 939

DENMARK
DESIGNERS GUILD DENMARK
Bukkeballevej 24
2960 Rungsted Kyst
Tel: (00 45 42) 864 480

EIRE
GERALDINE HUDSON INTERIOR
FURNISHINGS
2 Herbert Lane
Dublin 2
Tel: (00 35 31) 662 4648

FRANCE
DESIGNERS GUILD SARL
10 Rue Saint Nicolas
75012 Paris
Tel: (00 33 1) 44 67 80 70

FINLAND
INTERFURN OY AB
Ståhlbersvägen
00570 Helsinki
Tel: (00 35 80) 7001 7650

GERMANY
DESIGNERS GUILD GMBH
Sendlinger-Tor-Platz 6
80336 München
Tel: (00 49 89) 2311620

GREECE
PERSEFONE N DIAMANDAS
& CO EE
14 Filikis Eterias Square
GR-106 73 Athens
Tel: (00 30 1) 361 9266

HONG KONG
AVANT GARDE DESIGNS LIMITED
19th Floor Regency Centre
39 Wong Chuk Hang Road
Hong Kong
Tel: (00 852 2) 552 7533

ICELAND
BEZT LTD
Skolavorovstig 12 101
Reykjavik
Tel: (00 354) 551 2920

INDONESIA
PT CIPTA MERKURIUS
INTERNATIONAL
Jalan Abdul Muis No 24-26
Jakarta Pusat 10160
Tel: (00 62 21) 381 0968

ISRAEL
SEZAM LTD
255 Dizengoff Street
Shop 406 63117
Tel-Aviv
Tel: (00 972 3) 546 3521

ITALY
BLUE HOME DISTRIBUTION SPA
via Tevere 24
50019 Loc. Osmannoro
Sesto Fiorentino (FL)
Tel: (00 39 55) 311 795

JAPAN
FUJIE TEXTILE CO. LTD
No. 7-12 4-Chome Sendagaya
Shibuyaku Tokyo 151
Tel: (00 81 3) 3405 1312

KOREA
SOUTH SPRING INTERNATIONAL
CO LTD
Young Dong PO Box 344
Seoul 135-603
Tel: (00 82 2) 549 6701

KUWAIT
AL SEDRAH
M/S Abdulla Alomar Alyagout
PO Box 206 13003 Safat
Tel: (00 965) 264 9466

LEBANON
PERSPECTIVES SAL
PO Box 4198 Beirut
Tel: (00 961) 1334 120

MALAYSIA
RUFFLES FURNISHING
c/o Sinnan
F17/18 1st Floor
Plaza Yow Chuan
Jalan Tun Razak
50400 Kuala Lumper
Tel: (00 60 3) 242 8573

MEXICO
ARTELL SA DE CV
Calle 20 No 9
Colonia San Pedro de los Pinos
Mexico 03800 DF
Tel: (00 52 5) 272 2861

NETHERLANDS
WILHELMINE VAN AERSSEN
AGENTUREN
Amsterdamseweg 108-110
1182 HH Amstelveen
Tel: (00 31 20) 6405060

NEW ZEALAND
MOKUM TEXTILES LIMITED
11 Cheshire Street
Parnell Auckland 1
Tel: (00 64 9) 379 3041

NORWAY
DESIGN WORKS
PO Box 5019
Majorsteun 0301 Oslo 3
Tel: (00 47 22) 46 56 41

PHILIPPINES
JODY'S FABRICS INC
2nd Floor Lapuz Building
19 Pasay Road Makati
Metro Manila
Tel: (00 63 2) 843 58 32

POLAND
FUKIER S.C.
Rynek Starego Miasta 27
00-272 Warszawa
Tel: (00 48 22) 625 77 22

PORTUGAL
PEDROSO E OSORIO
Rua Fernao Lopes 409-2
4100 Oporto
Tel: (00 351 2) 617 1497

SAUDI ARABIA
AHMED G ALESAYI
PO Box 5651 Jeddah 21432
Tel: (00 966 2) 669 0071

SINGAPORE
LINEA TRE
402 Orchard Road
4-02/05 Delfi Orchard
Singapore 0923
Tel: (00 65) 734 5540

SOUTH AFRICA
H F HOME FABRICS LTD
60 Old Pretoria Road
Halfway House
Midrand, 1685
Johannesburg
Tel: (00 27 11) 805 0300

SPAIN
USERA USERA
Ayala 56 28001 Madrid
Tel: (010 34 1) 577 94 61

SWEDEN
TAPI
Kommend´rsgatan 22
114 48 Stockholm
Tel: (00 46 8) 661 0380

SWITZERLAND
DESIGNERS GUILD AG
Tel: 0848 808 718

THAILAND
SHEET'N SHADE CO LTD
344 Rama 3 Road
Bangklo Bangkorlaem
Bangkok 10120
Tel: (00 66 2) 289 4655-6

TURKEY
DIZAYN TEKSTIL DIS TIC LTD
Tesvikiye Atiye SK:7/4
AK AP 8200 Sisli Istanbul
Tel: (00 902 12) 247 3206

UNITED ARAB EMIRATES
AATI
PO Box 2623 Dubai
Tel: (00 971 4) 377 825

USA
Fabric and paper:
OSBORNE & LITTLE INC
979 Third Avenue - Suite 520
New York NY 10022
Tel: (00 1 212) 751 3333

Bed and bath:
DESIGNERS GUILD BED
AND BATH SHOWROOM
Regent Corporation
20th Floor 1185 6th Avenue
New York NY 10036
Tel: (00 1 212) 730 1800

©DESIGNERS GUILD™
is a registered trademark

Fabric, wallpaper, bed & bath and furniture directory

One-off furniture, ceramics and other commissioned work by artists and craftspeople that appear in the book are listed below and are available from the **Designers Guild Store, 267 Kings Road, London SW3 5EN.**

Designers Guild fabrics, wallpapers, bed and bath and furniture (which appear in **bold** in the following list) are available from the Designers Guild Store and from the stockists listed on pages 204-5. Kalamkari is a collection of wallpapers whose colours and textures correspond to the paint and plaster colours shown on the walls.

TRICIA GUILD'S HOUSE

Hall: Pages 17-23
Wall colours: **Kalamkari** Apple
Whitened plaster: **Kalamkari** Alabaster
Tom Dixon seagrass 'S' chairs
Blue amphora by Ralph Levy
Hand-blown glass and wirework vase

Conservatory: Pages 24-32
Wall colour: **Kalamkari** Ultramarine
Paul Anderson reclaimed oak table handmade for Designers Guild
Ajanta, kilim, handmade seagrass chairs and low table
Bandhani cotton printed fabric throw on chair
Ceramics: one-off ceramics by the following artists commissioned by Tricia Guild: Liz Hodges, Linda Hoffhines, Edla Griffiths, Ralph Levy, Henriette Gaillard, Lucy Greenaway
Orange and indigo cushion and throw in **Borghese** silk embroidered in string
Philippe Starck Mirto table and Lord Yo chairs

Sitting Room: Pages 40-9
Wall colour: **Kalamkari** Turquoise
Curtains in natural **Tullow** sackcloth and lime **Sakumari**, printed gold filigree on crushed cotton
Curl armchairs in shocking pink **Borghese** silk
Sofa in white **Killala** weave
Borghese silk cushions in orange and pink
Aripana printed cotton throw lined with **Tullow** sackcloth
Lime ceramic table by Ralph Levy to order
Sekordi handmade striped indigo kilim
Linda Hoffhines ceramic jug
Copper Papiro lights

Sitting Room: Pages 50-3
Wall colour: **Kalamkari** Turquoise
Hand-painted antique cupboard
Paint finish by Nick Garrett for Designers Guild
Duras sofa in orange **Borghese** silk
Balzac armchairs in natural **Killala** weave
Sekordi handmade striped indigo kilim

Study: Pages 54-7
Wall colour: **Kalamkari** Rouge
Turquoise ceramic top desk to order
Curl armchair in indigo **Borghese** silk
Patola handmade indigo kilim
Beechwood **Carugo** chair upholstered in lime **Saffa** chenille
Wool throw by Richard Womersley for Designers Guild

Kitchen: Pages 58-63
Wall colour: **Kalamkari** Alabaster and **Kalamkari** Apple
Curtains in pink **Kashipur** woven check
Hand-painted antique armoire

Blue and white Polish cappuccino cups, selection of olive oils, lime green kettle, table mats and napkins from Kitchen Department at Designers Guild

Dining Room: Pages 64-71
One-off handmade oak table and bench
Beechwood basic chair
Sofa in **Tillara** cerise, cushions in turquoise and orange **Borghese** silk
Throw in **Tullow** sackcloth by Lisa Vaughan
Loge leather chair and stool
Ceramic fireplace to order
Ceramic jugs by Edla Griffiths

Garden: Pages 71-2
Ceramic pond and kidney-shaped stools to order

Bedroom: Pages 80-7
Wall colour: **Kalamkari** Hyacinth
Curtains and bedcover in white **Mahé** crushed linen embroidered with string
Handcrafted metal bed
Curl armchairs in lime and white **Mahé** crushed linen
One-off handmade pink ceramic mirror
Cushions in cornflower and hyacinth **Tandragee** muslin

Bathroom: Pages 90-5
Curtains in white **Kilfinny** embroidered with string
Lime and natural cotton waffle towels and selection of soaps and bathroom accessories from Bed and Bath Department at Designers Guild
One-off lime ceramic fireplace to order
Ceramics by Linda Hoffhines

Small Guest Bedroom: Pages 96-7
Wall colour: **Kalamkari** Aqua
Wall painting by Janet and Paul Czainski
Metal Carmelit bed
Schiapparelli pink **Mahé** bedcover in crushed linen

Guest Room: Page 98
Wall colour: **Kalamkari** Tangerine
Wall painting by Janet and Paul Czainski
Hand-painted antique furniture
Pair of antique armchairs covered in pink **Milford** cotton check
Zinc bed with banner and bedcover in white **Mahé** crushed linen
Throw in turquoise **Mei P'ing** lined with **Tullow** sackcloth
Patola handmade kilim
Turquoise fireplace to order

Guest Bathroom: Page 100-1
Curtain in turquoise **Oola** cotton gauze
Waffle towel and bathroom accessories from Bed and Bath Department at Designers Guild

Guest Room: Pages 102-3
Wall colour: **Stucco** Malachite
Hand-painted antique furniture
One-off handmade ceramic mirror
Candlesticks by Liz Hodges
Throw and cushion in **Kashipur** turquoise cotton check

Blue Bathroom: Pages 104-5
Curtain in orange **Oola** cotton gauze
Cotton waffle towels from Bed and Bath Department at Designers Guild

TOWN HOUSE

Hall and Sitting Room: Pages 112-7
Wall colours: Hall - **Jhati** Cyclamen
Sitting Room - **Kalamkari** Hyacinth
Indigo and pink runner in hall by Jason Collingwood for Designers Guild
Curtain in **Jalapuri** checked silk
Trenton chairs in pink and lime **Nantua** damask
Nashville sofa in red and yellow striped **Lalitha** velvet
Curl chair in orange **Kota** cotton canvas
Manhattan sofa in lime **Kusumam** fabric
Patola handmade kilim
One-off candlesticks by Liz Hodges
Metal and slate topped low table from a selection

Kitchen and Dining Room: Pages 118-22
Wall colour: **Kalamkari** Plaster
Cherrywood Banca high stool
Sacramento sofa in natural **Hopsack**
Hand thrown terracotta flower pots from a selection
Loose covers on dining chairs: natural **Tullow** sackcloth, tied with string

Bedroom: Pages 122-5
Wall colour: **Kalamkari** Cornflower
Curtains in white **Mahé** crushed linen and **Jalapuri** silk check
Bedcover in blue **Ching Pei** printed on linen
Bedlinen: **Millville** and **Winthrop** appliqué sheet and pillowcases
Atlanta chair in **Tanda** cobalt stripe
Lime **Milford** cushion

Dressing Room: Pages 126-7
Wall colour: **Kalamkari** Cornflower
Blind in white **Mahé** crushed linen
Loose cover on **Newport** chair in pink **Mahé**
High bleached wood metal Pauvre table

ARTISAN'S TERRACE

Sitting Room - Pages 128-32
Wall colour: **Kalamkari** Pale Lime
Blinds: **Jalapuri** mauve and lime check silk
Washed **Jalapuri** silk throw lined in **Tullow** sackcloth
Cushions on sofa in **Cashel**, **Jalapuri** silk and **Mahé** crushed linen

Turquoise **Aripana** throw, lined in **Tullow** sackcloth
Hand-painted antique cupboard
Runner on table in washed emerald **Jalapuri** silk
Napkins in lime **Mahé** crushed linen
Ceramics by Tilly Stacey-Young

Bedroom: Pages 134-5
Wall colour: **Aviz** Aqua
Curtains in natural **Mahé** crushed linen and turquoise **Oola** cotton gauze
Bedcover in turquoise **Mei-Ping** printed on linen
Throw in **Cashel** sackcloth
Lime **Oola** and white **Mahé** curtain on page 137

HOME AS A HAVEN

Sitting Room: Pages 144-9
Wall colour: **Kalamkari** white
Curtains in white **Mahé** crushed linen and **Tullow** sackcloth
Manhattan sofa and floor cushions in white **Killala** weave
Cushions on sofa in red and natural **Mahé** crushed linen
Bleached wood and metal Pauvre tables
Hand-painted red and white antique cupboard
Lord Yo chairs by Philippe Starck and Adelino table

Bedroom: Pages 150-1
Curtains in pink **Milford** cotton check
Metal Carmelit bed
Banner on bed in pink **Tandragee** muslin
Throw in orange **Ralston** stripe lined with pink **Litchfield** check
Bedlinen: embroidered red **Milroy** and appliqué **Redmond**
Pink ceramic top desk to order

NEW YORK

Sitting Room and Hall: Pages 152-7
Wall colour: **Kalamkari** Tangerine and Turquoise
Curtains in lime **Oola** cotton gauze and **Tullow** sackcloth
Sofa in striped **Saffa** lime chenille
Cushions in **Tullow** sackcloth and red **Mahé** crushed linen
Chairs in **Lapundra** lime and turquoise stripe
Throws in washed red **Jalapuri** silk and **Odhni** lime printed cotton
Ceramics on table by Linda Hoffhines

Bedroom: Pages 158-9
Wall colour: **Pushpa** Almond
Curtains in lime **Mei Ping** printed on crushed linen and **Tulsk** weave
Bedcover in lime **Mahé** crushed linen
Bedlinen: yellow **Saxton** check and **Millville** appliquéd cotton

Index

author's acknowledgements

With much appreciation to the following artists, craftspeople and suppliers: Paul Anderson Bar Italia Mick Brady James Burnett-Stewart Cappellini Julian Cloke John Cullen Lighting Janet and Paul Czainski John Derrian Tom Dixon John Fennell Alex Frankl Henriette Gaillard Nick Garrett Lucy Greenaway Edla Griffiths Liz Hodges Linda Hoffhines Homeier UK Peter Keegan Ralph Levy Loom Company Terry Lynch Maroeska Metz Molesley Refridgeration Sean Oakes Orsino Papers & Paints A. H. Peck Flooring Lawrence Pidgeon / Alternative Plans Pont de la Tour Pulbrook & Gould Rainbow Leisure River Café Valerie Roy SCP SKK Tilly Stacey-Young Lucy Stentiford Sally Storey/Lighting Design Summerill & Bishop Linda Thorn Unidec Lisa Vaughn Wandsworth Electrical Alan Warburton Wild At Heart Melanie Williams Conroy Winter Richard Womersley

thank you

We would like to thank the following publishers for kind permission to use quotations from their publications:

Aristotle, Politics, translated by T.A. Sinclair, Penguin, 1981

Italo Calvino, Invisible Cities, Secker & Warburg, 1981

Richard Rogers, "The Reith Lectures" from Cities for a Small Planet, Faber & Faber, 1996

Harvey Sherlock, Cities are Good for Us, Palladin Press, 1991

Peter Jukes, A Shout in the Street, Faber & Faber, 1990

Anthony Vidler, The Scenes on the Street, MIT Press, Massachusetts, 1978

Franz Kafka, The Transformation (Metamorphosis) and Other Stories, translated by Malcolm Pasley, Penguin, 1992

John Berger, About Looking, Penguin, 1980

P B Shelley Poems and Prose, Everyman,1995

Charles Baudelaire, The Poems in Prose, Anvil editions, 1991

Lisa Lovatt-Smith, Paris Interiors, Taschen, 1994

Thomas Carlyle, On Heroes, Hero-Worship and the Heroic in History, University of Nebraska, 1966